Best
Classroom
Management
Practices
for Reaching All Learners

Other Corwin Press Books by Randi Stone

Best Teaching Practices for Reaching All Learners: What Award-Winning Classroom Teachers Do, 2004

What?! Another New Mandate? What Award-Winning Teachers Do When School Rules Change, 2002

Best Practices for High School Classrooms: What Award-Winning Secondary Teachers Do, 2001

Best Classroom Practices: What Award-Winning Elementary Teachers Do, 1999

New Ways to Teach Using Cable Television: A Step-by-Step Guide, 1997

Best
Classroom
Management
Practices
for Reaching All Learners

What Award-Winning Classroom Teachers Do

Randi Stone

CORWIN PRESS
A SAGE Publications Company
Thousand Oaks, California

For information:

Corwin Press
A Sage Publications Company
2455 Teller Road
Thousand Oaks, California 91320
www.corwinpress.com

Sage Publications Ltd.
1 Oliver's Yard
55 City Road
London EC1Y 1SP
United Kingdom

Sage Publications India Pvt. Ltd.
B-42, Panchsheel Enclave
Post Box 4109
New Delhi 110 017 India

Printed in the United States of America

Library of Congress Cataloging-in-Publication Data

Best classroom management practices for reaching all learners: What award-winning classroom teachers do / [edited by] Randi Stone.
        p. cm.
Includes index.
ISBN 1-4129-0969-4 (cloth)—ISBN 1-4129-0970-8 (pbk.)
    1. Classroom management—United States. I. Stone, Randi.
LB3011.B53 2005
371.102′4—dc22
                                                                2004026181

This book is printed on acid-free paper.

05   06   07   08   09   10   9   8   7   6   5   4   3   2   1

Acquisitions Editor:	Faye Zucker
Editorial Assistant:	Gem Rabanera
Production Editor:	Melanie Birdsall
Copy Editor:	Elizabeth Budd
Typesetter:	C&M Digitals (P) Ltd.
Proofreader:	Cheryl Rivard
Indexer:	Michael Ferreira
Cover Designer:	Michael Dubowe

To my precious daughter, Blair.

Contents

Preface

This book surveys award-winning teachers around the country about the best classroom management practices they use to reach all learners. This instant network in your hands is a one-of-a-kind educational resource.

▧ Who Should Read This Book

This book is for K–12 educators who would like to know how the best teachers handle classroom management. It puts a network at your fingertips, providing names, postal addresses, and e-mail addresses of the teachers who share their strategies.

▧ Acknowledgments

I thank all the generous teachers across the country who shared their insights. Grateful acknowledgment is also made to the contributors for special permission to use their material.

About the Author

Randi Stone is a graduate of Clark University, Boston University, and Salem State College. She completed her doctorate in education from the University of Massachusetts, Lowell. She is the author of seven books with Corwin Press, including her latest publication, *Best Teaching Practices for Reaching All Learners.* She lives with her husband, Bryan, and daughter, Blair, in Keene, New Hampshire.

About the Contributors

Sharon Andrews, Teacher, Grade 5
  Challenge Center at Mark Twain Elementary
  315 West 27th Street
  Sioux Falls, South Dakota 57108
  School Telephone Number: (605) 367-4560
  E-mail: andresha@sf.k12.sd.us

Number of Years Teaching: 11
Awards: Presidential Award for Excellence in
         Mathematics and Science Teaching, 2003
         Huber Scholarship for Outstanding Doctoral Student in
         Curriculum and Instruction, University of South Dakota,
         Vermillion, 1999

Keith Ballard, Director of Mariachi Music
  Montgomery Middle School
  1051 Picador Boulevard
  San Diego, California 92154
  School Telephone Number: (619) 662-4000
  E-mail: keith.ballard@suhsd.k12.ca.us

Number of Years Teaching: 9
Awards: Milken Family Foundation National Educator Award, 2003
         Arizona State University "Hall of Fame" Inductee, 2003
         CA Teacher's Association Cesar Chavez Human Rights
         Award, 2003

Zoma A. Barrett, Computer Technology Teacher, Grade 8; Mathematics Teacher, Grade 6; Advanced Technology Teacher, Grades 6–8
   Salem Middle School
   1001 North Harrison Street
   Salem, Indiana 47167
   School Telephone Number: (812) 883-3808
   E-mail: zbarrett@salemschools.com
Number of Years Teaching: 7
Awards: Milken Family Foundation National Educator Award, 2003
            Salem Community Schools You Make the Difference Award
            for Outstanding Teaching and Dedication, 2003

Cliff B. Barrineau, Geometry, Grade 8; Algebra II, Grade 9; Pre-Calculus and SAT Math Preparation, Grades 11 and 12; Using Calculators, Grades 11 and 12
   Dreher High School
   701 Adger Road
   Columbia, South Carolina 29205
   School Telephone Number: (803) 787-7226
   E-mail: Cbarrineau@richlandone.org
Number of Years Teaching: 19
Awards: Milken Family Foundation National Educator Award, 2003
            Hand Middle School Teacher of the Year and
                Finalist for Richland School District One
                Teacher of the Year, 1998–1999
            Rotary Club Honorary Paul Harris Fellowship, 1998

Dano Beal, Teacher, Highly Capable "Spectrum" Program, Grades 1/2 Multiage
   Lafayette Elementary, Seattle Public Schools
   2645 SW California Avenue
   Seattle, Washington 98116
   School Telephone Number: (206) 252-9500
   E-mail: dabeal@seattleschools.org
Number of Years Teaching: 14
Awards: Disney Hand American Teacher Awards Honoree, 2003
            Washington State Science Teacher of the Year, 1994
            U.S. Space Foundation "Master Teacher" Recognition 1994

Jesus "Jesse" Bernal, Spanish Teacher, Grades 9–12
Garden City High School—USD 457
1412 N. Main
Garden City, Kansas 67846
School Telephone Number: (620) 276-5170
E-mail: jbernal@gckschools.com

Number of Years Teaching: 15
Awards: Milken Family Foundation National Educator Award, 2003
    League of United Latin American Citizens:
    Man of the Year, 1999

Carrie Jane Carpenter, Language Arts Teacher, Grades 7–8, and
Technology School Coordinator
Hugh Hartman Middle School
2105 W. Antler Avenue
Redmond, Oregon 97756
School Telephone Number: (541) 923-4840
E-mail: ccarpent@redmond.k12.or.us

Number of Years Teaching: 10
Awards: Oregon's Teacher of the Year, 2003
    Intel Teach to the Future Master Teacher, 2000–2002

Patricia F. Clark, Academic Intervention Services Teacher, Kindergarten,
Grades 1–2
Alden Terrace Elementary School
1835 North Central Avenue
North Valley Stream, New York 11580
School Telephone Number: (516) 285-8310
E-mail: wesynch@optonline.net

Number of Years Teaching: 22
Awards: Scott Foresman National Teacher Award, 2000
    National Teachers Hall of Fame, 2000

Carolyn M. Daniels, Homeroom/Literature, Grade 6; Science, Grades
5–8; Computer, Grades K–8
Our Lady of Mount Carmel School
115 Lewis Avenue

Meriden, Connecticut 06451
School Telephone Number: (203) 235-2959
E-mail: our.lady.mt.carml@snet.net

Number of Years Teaching: 6
Awards: Who's Who Among America's Teachers, 2004
Scott Foresman and The National
Teacher's Hall of Fame National Teacher
Award, 2000

Maria I. Davis, Intermediate Teacher
Bramble Academy
4324 Homer Avenue
Cincinnati, Ohio 45227
School Telephone Number: (513) 363-9600
E-mail: riaidavis1@hotmail.com

Number of Years Teaching: 11
Awards: Who's Who Among America's Teachers, 2004
Scott Foresman National Teacher
Award, 2000

Joyce Dunn, Teacher, Grade 1
Shanksville Stonycreek School District
PO Box 128
Shanksville, Pennsylvania 15560
School Telephone Number: (814) 267-7140
E-mail: jdunn@sssd.com

Number of Years Teaching: 36
Award: Pennsylvania Teacher of the Year, 2003

Mary Eby, Teacher, Grade 2
Woodbine Elementary School
Woodbine, Iowa 51579
School Telephone Number: (712) 647-2440
E-mail: ebybob@pionet.net

Number of Years Teaching: 21
Award: Winner of Unsung Heroes Award Sponsored
by ING

Deborah Gordon, Teacher, Grade 3
Madison Simis School
7302 North 10th Street
Phoenix, Arizona 85020
School Telephone Number: (602) 664-7300
E-mail: dgordon@msd38.org

Number of Years Teaching: 17
Awards: Presidential Award for Excellence in Mathematics
and Science Teaching, 2002
You Make a Difference Award, Madison School
District, 1999
Madison School District Teacher of the Year, 1995–1996

Randy Heite
Kingsley Elementary
2300 Greenbay Road
Evanston, Illinois 60201
School Telephone Number: (847) 859-8400

Award: Disney Hand Teacher Award Honoree, 2003

Pauline H. Jacroux, Teacher, Grade 1
Aikahi Elementary School
281 Ilihau Street
Kailua, Hawaii 96734
School Telephone Number: (808) 254-7944
E-mail: phjacroux@earthlink.net

Number of Years Teaching: 19
Awards: Disney American Teacher Award, 2002–2003
Who's Who Among America's Teachers, 1998

Chris Laster, Science Specialist, Grades 4–5 (self-contained special
education inclusion, Grade 5, for eight years previously)
Russell Elementary
3920 South Hurt Road
Smyrna, Georgia 30082
School Telephone Number: (770) 437-5937
E-mail: krislast@bellsouth.net

Number of Years Teaching: 11
Awards: USA Today All Star Teaching Team, 2003
American Institute of Aeronautics and Astronautics,
National Educator Achievement Award, 2002
Georgia Science Teacher of the Year, 2002

Cathy Lutz, Teacher, Grade 1
Madison Station Elementary
2109 Main Street
Madison, Mississippi 39110
School Telephone Number: (601) 856-6246
E-mail: cathylutz@bellsouth.net

Number of Years Teaching: 15
Awards: PAEMST: Presidential Award for Excellence in
Mathematics and Science Teaching
National Board Certified Teacher:
Early Childhood, Generalist
President MCTM: Mississippi Council
of Teachers of Mathematics

John McCleary, Principal
Ward Middle School
PO Box 338
Ordway, Colorado 81063
E-mail: mcclearyj1@hotmail.com

Number of Years Teaching: 7
Award: Milken Award for Educators

Gail McGoogan, Teacher, Grade 4, Vertical Teaching Team
Narcoossee Community School
2700 N. Narcoossee Road
St. Cloud, Florida 34771
School Telephone Number: (407) 891-6600
E-mail: mcgoogag@aol.com or mcgoogag@osceola.k12.fl.us

Number of Years Teaching: 10
Awards: Disney Hand Elementary Teacher of the Year, 2003
Disney Teacherrific Special Judges Award, 2001
National Board Certified Teacher, 1999

Cynthia R. Murray, Business Teacher, Grades 9–12; School-to-Work
Coordinator
   Covington High School
   73030 Lion Drive
   Covington, Louisiana 70433
   School Telephone Number: (985) 871-9095
   E-mail: cynthia.murray@stpsb.org
Number of Years Teaching: 25
Award: ING Unsung Heroes Award, 2003

Teresa Morton Owens, Teacher, Grade 5
   Susan Moore Elementary School
   3996 Susan Moore Road
   Blountsville, Alabama 35031
   School Telephone Number: (205) 466-5844
   E-mail: towens@blountcountyschools.net
Awards: Unsung Heroes Award, ING Corporation, 2003–2004
           Winner, Connections Program Grant, SMARTer
              Kids Foundation, 2002–2004
           NBPTS—Middle Child Generalist, 2001

Veronique Paquette, Teacher, Grade 2
   Kenroy Elementary School
   601 North Jonathan
   East Wenatchee, Washington 98802
   School Telephone Number: (509) 884-1443
Award: Washington Teacher of the Year, 2003

John P. Pieper, Elementary Teacher, Grade 5
   Webster Stanley Elementary School
   915 Hazel Street
   Oshkosh, Wisconsin 54901
   School Telephone Number: (920) 424-0460
   E-mail: jpieper@new.rr.com
Number of Years Teaching: 22
Awards: Disney American Teacher Award Honoree, 2003
           Citation by the State of Wisconsin Legislature
              for Excellence in Education, 2002

Beverly R. Plein, Family and Consumer Science Teacher, Technology Facilitator, Grades 7–12

Cresskill Junior Senior High School

1 Lincoln Drive

Cresskill, New Jersey 07626

School Telephone Number: (201) 567-5479

E-mail: bplein@cresskillboe.k12.nj.us

Number of Years Teaching: 18

Awards: Milken Family Foundation National Educator Award, 2003
Teacher of the Year, Cresskill
School District, 1994

Pam Roller, Teacher, Grade 2

Galveston Elementary School

401 South Maple Street

Galveston, Indiana 46932

School Telephone Number: (574) 699-6687

E-mail: rollerp@sesc.k12.in.us

Number of Years Teaching: 30

Awards: Disney American Teacher Award Honoree, 2003
Cass County Conservation Teacher of the Year, 1997
NASA/NSTA Newest, 1993

Eric Stemle, English, Grades 9–12

Evanston High School

1615 Cheyenne Drive

Evanston, Wyoming 82930

School Telephone Number: (307) 789-0757

E-mail: estemle@msn.com

Number of Years Teaching: 28

Awards: NEA Foundation Award for Teaching Excellence
(Wyoming Awardee), 2003
Wyoming Teacher of the Year, 2003
Wal-Mart Teacher of the Year (Sweetwater
County), 1999

Betsy Ann Wandishin, Head Teacher, Grade 5
Crooked River Elementary School
1437 Poland Spring Road
Casco, Maine 04015
School Telephone Number: (207) 627-4291
E-mail: Bwandes1@maine.rr.com

Number of Years Teaching: 19
Award: Maine Teacher of the Year, 2003

CHAPTER 1

The Buck Reward System

Maria I. Davis

Cincinnati, Ohio

"**M**s. Davis, can I go to the bathroom?" asked Janice.

"No, *I* gotta use it!" demands Gary.

"Is we gonna do math or reading now?" asked Missy, politely.

"I need a Band-Aid, Ms. Davis. See." (As Ashley tugs at my blouse.)

"Kirk hit me in my head!" shouted Fred.

Thinking: *It is now 8:02 and I still have six more hours of this? How on earth am I gonna get through this day?*

"Yes, you may go to the bathroom, Janice, but don't waste time. Gary, I don't know what 'it' is, but if you are referring to the bathroom, then you may use 'it' when Janice comes back, and I'd really like for you to say 'have to' instead of 'gotta,' okay? And Missy, did you say 'Is we'?"

"Are we," she says.

"Look at the schedule, sweetie. And Ashley, You said you *need* a Band-Aid, well, I *need* to win the lotto!"

"Ms. Daaaavis, you know what I mean," whines Ashley.

"Yes, I do know what you mean, but when you would like something, ask me, don't tell me. I will get a Band-Aid in a moment, but please sit down, and Fred, don't start that nonsense. Kirk isn't even here yet!"

This is a typical morning with my fifth-grade students in my urban neighborhood classroom. They are in constant conversation with me or one another, or simply having a private conversation within themselves. They are up and down, in and out of the closet, and someone is always sharpening a pencil! They always need something, and those needs must be met immediately. I know I hear "Ms. Davis" more than 100 times a day, and I feel that to be a good teacher, I must respond each and every time—well, not exactly.

I learned a rewards system years ago from a colleague by the name of Ms. Simmons. I adapted her idea and tweaked it to fit my needs and the needs of my students. This Buck System is not only a means of rewarding my students for positive behaviors, making smart choices, or for giving exemplary answers in class, but it also controls disruptive bathroom breaks and breaking class rules and discourages many of my students from yelling out answers during instruction.

For starters, I use play money that has my face on it. In the past eight years, I have used currency from 1 "buck" to 1,000 "bucks" and have tested their effectiveness with students from Grades 4 through 8. I never use all the amounts at the same time. I usually choose two amounts and stay with them the entire year. Last quarter, I introduced a larger "buck" to keep students interested during the last two months of the school year.

I use bucks to reward my students for various positive behaviors. The system is implemented the first day of school with little introduction. I simply give out bucks to students who remember to raise their hand, who show respect to a peer, or to that one student who is listening when the others just won't shut their mouths! "Thank you so much, Todd, for showing me that you are ready," I say, as I hand him five bucks. This *always* captures the attention of others.

As the day progresses, I try to find a reason to give every child at least one buck. Some may have a five, and others may have a twenty.

Of course, by midmorning, everyone is starting to ask questions. "What is this for?" "Why'd she give him twenty?" "What are we gonna do with these?" When the time is just right, the Buck System is introduced. I begin by asking the students, "When did you get that?" or "Why did I give that to you?" At first there is little response, but usually a sibling of a former student has all the answers—well, almost.

"We get these when we do something good. She doesn't have to give them to us, but she thinks they are fun. You have to keep up with your own bucks just like it is real money, and you gotta save them up so you can buy something on Friday. She gets stuff like pencils, paper, pop, candy, or computer time, and if you got a lot of 'em, you can buy lunch with the teacher! She orders pizza and pop, and you get to talk to her the whole time. If you lose them, oh, well. Plus, my brother told me that Ms. Davis will take them if you get on her nerves, or if she has to keep saying your name, and that it cost fifty bucks to go use 'it,' I mean, go to the restroom. Ain't that right, Ms. Davis?"

After this condensed and somewhat inaccurate account of the Buck System, I try to mend the mistakes and get my students more interested in it.

"Thank you, Mattie. Well, almost. Let me clarify a few things. The bucks are given for positive behaviors and making smart choices, and I give them out when I think you did a fantastic job on something. Some days I may give out a lot of bucks, and other days I may not. If you want to know how well you are doing, count your bucks, but not during instruction, or I will take them. If you have had a great week, you may have a lot of bucks on Friday. However, if you missed an assignment, interrupted me while I was talking, or decided to get out of your seat without permission, you may not have many bucks. But guess what? Next week you start fresh."

"You mean we *gotta* buy something on Friday? And if we don't, we gotta give 'em back to you?"

"No," I continue. "Once you earn your bucks, they are yours, although I may take them, but I'll explain that in a moment. What I meant was that some weeks you may get a lot of bucks, but other weeks you may not. That's okay. It's up to you. You will be able to tell on Friday what type of week you have had. Bucks are not to be used for any other purpose than for what we use them for here in the classroom.

They shouldn't be used at lunch to buy someone's food. If you abuse them and I find out, I will charge you."

"Charge us? What do that mean?" asked Kevin.

"Say that again, Kevin," I reply.

"What do that—I mean, what *does* that mean, charge?"

"Good question. You know that you get bucks for certain behaviors; well, I can take bucks, too. You know my rules and expectations. They are posted, and we discussed them earlier. If you break a rule, you have to pay me. I take the entire class on a restroom break once a day, but if you need to go again, you have to pay. That way, you are less likely to waste time by asking to go."

"What?" shouted Andy.

"Aw, man!" says Fred.

"That ain't fair," mumbles Gary.

"That will be five bucks apiece. Andy, Fred, and Gary, you know that you don't yell out in my room, we just talked about that."

"Aww, that's funny! She got y'all," laughed Jacob. (By the way, Jacob has already earned fifty bucks today. He is bright and opinionated, but also very loud.)

"But guess what, Jacob, I got you too! You owe me fifteen bucks."

The room has hushed. Not a sound. Thinking: *I love this. He is going to be a little upset with me, but he has enough bucks that it won't matter. Jacob will think twice next time he is ready to laugh at others.* Just then Jacob reluctantly shuffles up to me with his head down and hands me fifteen bucks without protest.

"As I was saying, when you break a rule or interrupt or disturb others, I will charge you. I sometimes forget, but believe me, your classmates will remind me. Any questions?"

"How much *does* the stuff cost?" asks Kevin.

Well, you don't buy things, you bid on them. We have Silent Auctions on Friday afternoons.

"Does anyone know what an auction is?" Heads turn, and some eyes roll as Mattie raises her hand.

"My brother told me that you set up all the things on a table during lunch. When we come back, we can look at all the stuff and pick out in our heads what we want, but we might not get it. And you can't talk during auction. That's why you call it silent auction."

"Thank you, Mattie, but you still did not answer my question. What is an auction?"

Jacob, who is no longer giving me the evil eye, raises his hand. "An auction is when items are sold to the kid who wants to pay the most bucks for it. You don't set the price, we do."

"Excellent, Jacob. Here you go." Another twenty is handed to him. Jacob takes it and gives it a peck.

Helpful Tips

The Buck System is a simple way to control certain behaviors and reward students on a daily basis. I pass them out during instruction, in the hall, and any time I think a behavior should be rewarded. I make it clear to my students that I don't ever *have* to reward them for what is expected of them, but using the bucks is my choice. Items can range from nickel candies and school supplies to the most popular one, lunch with the teacher. Initially, auctions may seem expensive, but be creative and smart. Don't start off big, or the students will always expect big items, but remember to have at least one really "good" thing each time. Hold auctions monthly if weekly seems too often. My family members, friends, and colleagues offer items to me all the time. Take anything and everything someone gives you. You save a lot of money doing this.

Don't give out too many bucks, or they will lose their value. Be selective on how and when to use them. For students that challenge you daily, try to "pay" them for every single positive thing that they do. This way, when you have to charge them, they can pay. It may seem unfair, but trust me, it works out in the long run. These students will miss the first few auctions, but when they start to control their behavior and have bucks to spend, they will be angels on auction day.

My students have included a wide range of unique personalities and varying abilities. I have used the bucks every year regardless of the demographics of my class. Students learn the value of money and how to count money, and they learn to budget it as well.

They learn that immediate gratification is good, but having the ability to save for that one special item is awesome.

I have shared this system with many colleagues. Sometimes they buy into it, other times they pass. I know the Buck System is nothing new. I have met a lot of teachers who use similar reward systems. However, make it your own; make it part of your daily routine. It should not be a hassle or too intrusive. Have fun with your reward system. The more you enjoy it, the more your students will as well.

Using bucks as part of teaching may seem silly, complicated, or a waste to some, but my students either learn to be respectful or they pay. I don't have to search for a quick punishment or give threats when minor incidents occur because they automatically know their consequence: They pay bucks. The amount of money I spend for my students for auction or lunch with the teacher is worth every cent because the buck system makes my day more enjoyable—and sometimes even more tolerable.

CHAPTER 2

Managing With Silence and More

Carolyn M. Daniels

Meriden, Connecticut

"**S**he's waiting. Everybody, she's waiting!" is a phrase you will hear throughout the many classes I teach, and I love it. I stand in the classroom, glare at the students with my serious, teacher glare, and wait. One student quiets down, then another, and another. It may take a few minutes, and on tough days, it may take a few minutes longer, but eventually all students are silent, and that silence is golden. I know my students are ready to hear and listen.

In the beginning of the year, I explain to my students, in Grades K–8, I will not shush, clap, ring a bell, or yell to get their attention. I clearly articulate to them that I will just stand, and wait. And wait. And wait. My students quickly come to understand that I will wait all period for them, if necessary, to calm down, focus, and prepare for the lesson. Sometimes, while I am waiting, I will tally the passing minutes on the board, which allows the class to see the length of time it took them to focus. Over time, the students and I race to beat the minutes recorded on the board. This becomes a good lesson in telling time. Sometimes I love to stand in front of the class and observe, listen, and learn about them. My students, however, don't know that this is my ulterior motive. Students see this as the time to quiet down and pay attention because that is what I have taught them, and they *hate* when I fall silent. It absolutely drives them nuts!

Another technique I use with all my students is "Eyes on Me at Three." Any time I need to get my students' attention quickly, either to give a direction or to make an announcement, I call out this phrase, and then slowly count to three. With my younger students, I hold up my fingers as I say the numbers to give them a visual cue as well. My older students joke that three is the highest number that I can count to, but even they have learned to focus on me at three. I can then deliver whatever direction is necessary because the students are silent and focused.

The last technique I use persuades my students to listen and act on my directions. After I wait or count to three, I instruct the students to put their hands on their heads. My students enjoy this, and I benefit by knowing they are following my directions. In computer class, for example, I have students put their hands on their heads when they have logged on and are ready for their CDs, raise their hands and point to open the CD-ROM, and change places with their partners to take turns. The students quietly focus on my verbal directions in anticipation of their next movement, and I am able to complete a visual sweep of the room and assess their progress. They are engaged, eager to listen and learn, and are having fun, too!

The performer Paul Simon can captivate a concert crowd by singing his classic song "Sounds of Silence." I myself am content to wait. And count. And wait some more. My goal is for my students to hear me. I know that once they hear me, I can reach them, and teach them.

Helpful Tips

- Smile and never let them see you sweat!
- You never know what students are going to like, and neither do they, so always give them what they need, not what they want. You'll never be disappointed.
- Love what you do, and your students will love what you do, too.

CHAPTER 3

Beginning the Journey With the Challenging Students

Patricia F. Clark

North Valley Stream, New York

T hroughout the years of teaching, it seems we've all had our share of challenging or disruptive students. You know the ones I mean, those children who bully others, have numerous outbursts during the day, cheat, lie, steal, and even threaten or use physical violence. You can probably visualize them and recall their names even before you can name the well-behaved, highly motivated, and academically solid students! The former are the ones who challenge us the most, sap our energy, and purge us of all those strategies that we've stored over the years. These are the children whom we probably love the most because they need the most love. It takes a special type of fortitude to deal with them successfully.

The feelings of anguish I had regarding one particularly troubled student who was in my very large first-grade class several years ago surfaced again just recently. I found him on the floor outside my room weeping. My mind raced back as I recalled his first day in my class. He stabbed me with a pencil within the first hour and proceeded to turn the composition of the class upside down. I was scared. I remember vividly not wanting to return to the classroom after lunch! I made a firm mental commitment to myself and to the class that I would turn my fear into a positive attitude and create a win–win situation for him and for the rest of us. It was only the beginning of a long journey: empowerment— teaching him to make better choices more of the time rather than a struggle for power between us.

Where and how do you begin this journey? First, there must be an understanding between and among students and teacher. A well-planned daily routine is paramount because it creates a feeling of safety, which is a basic need. Flexibility must also have a place. Class rules, communally developed, are imperative. There must be some expectations of mutual respect and how that is reached. There must be consistency as well. The classroom must be constructivist in nature allowing the children to work in many types of cooperative groups. They have to be taught how to work on problems as they arise.

It is necessary to attempt the identification of some sources of behavior anomalies. Some students act out because of a need for power, and we can't engage in a struggle. We have to admonish, gently and firmly, a child who can be volatile. We must be resilient, consistent, and patient. There must be established consequences for behaviors that do not conform to classroom rules. We cannot let a child push our buttons, or the child will prevail. The other students in class must also be empowered to handle situations with this type of child so that they do not become victimized. Sometimes it is better to remove the rest of the class than it is to try to remove an out-of-control child!

With this in mind, as teachers, we must recognize that the behavior students choose can arise from another need: the need to belong. Some students want to be acknowledged so badly that they don't care if they achieve this through positive or negative attention. The latter never ceases to amaze me! Whether students ultimately make good decisions or poor ones lies, to a great degree, in our ability to guide them before they make a poor choice. They must be made to feel capable of doing the classroom tasks; they must feel connected to the group; they must believe that their contributions are worthwhile; and, finally, they must believe that their positive behavior matters to the well-being of the whole group. The group cares.

Some students act out because of the fear of failure; we can modify assignments or accept work in smaller increments until they fulfill an assignment. We may allow a student to have more time on task. We can give a second chance to succeed by completing or retaking a test or project. We can assign peer tutors or buddy children with older students who can help with academics and provide positive role models. We must also model, remodel, and scaffold. Another approach is to plan an extra few minutes a day to spend giving minilessons or suggestions in a small group or even one-on-one. At times, a big success builds on a series of smaller ones. Therefore, we must capitalize on the feelings of self-worth that success can engender.

Sometimes even though we endeavor to make students feel connected and regardless of the success they experience, a backslide may occur. Perhaps an incident unrelated to school can be the cause of anger a student displays. A problem can flare at recess or in art, music, or gym class, and we must be prepared to handle this with sensitivity. Overreaction will never help. Trying to anticipate triggers is daunting. The child must be forgiven and allowed to regain his or her status within the class; the student's self-esteem must be fostered. We must tolerate mistakes unless there is an element of danger involved for that student or others. We have to encourage the student so that he or she is able to get back on track.

We must be cognizant of the chain of command within the school. How are problematic situations handled where you work? Are there experienced colleagues with whom you can brainstorm? Does your school have behavior contracts? Are there psychologists or social workers whom you can call on in emergencies? Is there a dean of discipline? Many of the decisions you make may depend on what is already standard operating procedure.

Last of all, knowing when and how to involve parents is essential. Teachers must make allowances for the feelings of the parents of this type of child, because these parents probably hear few good reports.

We are often quick to call a parent with a concern about the child's poor judgment, but how often do we remember to call or write a note to celebrate a good or positive effort? Are there any concrete ways to involve parents more actively in the educational process that will be beneficial for their child? Provide insight rather than indictments whenever possible. A positive relationship with parents helps; an adversarial one does not.

Learning from the past, together with much self-reflection, makes subsequent issues more manageable. There are no miracles, just a solid, steady dose of old-fashioned common sense!

Helpful Tips

- Anticipate problem times by having a plan of action.
- Keep an analytical log of triggers.
- Ease transitions within the room.
- Keep the child closer to you than to peers with whom there are issues.
- Pick your battles—there are times to act and times to overlook.
- Try to stay calm and in control of your emotions.
- Choose a key phrase, gesture, or a tap on the desk to redirect attention.
- Be quick to give genuine praise, a wink, or a thumbs-up for good effort.
- Be consistent, firm, and fair.
- Give a second chance whenever possible.
- Look for and applaud the child's talents and allow these to be shared.
- Stay positive and build on all positives in the class.
- Be careful not to jump to conclusions.
- Provide verbal signals a few minutes in advance of the end of activities.
- Use concrete directions.
- Don't be afraid to seek advice.
- Involve parents whenever possible.
- Be reflective.

CHAPTER **4**

Using a Student Information Notebook

Betsy Ann Wandishin

Casco, Maine

"**M**rs. Roberts, you have a phone call in the office on Line 1," blares the intercom in your building. It is 3:15, and the students have just left. Your blood runs cold because you know it is the angry parent who sent you a scathing note that morning warning you to be ready for a phone call after school. You sigh as you trudge to the phone, thinking about the many calls you have had with this same parent. None of them seem productive, and they always go exactly the same way. The parent expresses her frustration in an angry tirade, and you waste all your energies defending yourself. Somehow, the parent always manages to bring up everything but what is really important: her daughter and the fact that she is not achieving her potential. The following strategies will outline ways to effectively organize communications with parents over the phone and in face-to-face conferences to focus all participants on what is most important: the student.

- Before school even begins, obtain a large binder and organize it with a tab folder for every student in your classroom.
- Make copies of emergency information sheets that go to the office, so that you have all telephone, cell phone, and pager numbers as well as e-mail addresses for every child's parent or guardian. These should be placed in the binder for easy access to communicate with parents.
- Other items to include in the binder are any interest or multiple intelligence surveys done to get to know students at the beginning of the year, copies of assessment results, notes from parents, and copies of your responses.
- Include blank copies of the Parent Call Worksheet and blank copies of the Parent Conference Planning and Note Sheet. This notebook should be kept in a convenient place so that if a parent calls or you have set up a parent meeting, it is always available with complete and updated information for every student.
- The purpose of the notebook and worksheets is to keep you, the teacher, focused and on track with parents when you are making those valuable communications about the students with whom you work. Oftentimes, conversations with parents can get off track when other students or issues enter the conversation. The Parent Call Worksheet and the Parent Conference Planning and Note Sheet keep the communication focused and on track because of your prior efforts to organize your thoughts and plan before these meetings or conversations.

When you have organized in such a fashion, it is very easy to get back on track by referring to your notes and sticking to the topic. In the long run, everyone involved in the communication is getting what they deserve—updated, concise information about the student and a chance to be heard. The Student Information Notebook is also a valuable tool for completing report cards and conferencing with other teachers and for use in special education meetings. Keep copies of all communications about each student in your notebook, and you will find that this becomes an indispensable part of your planning and reporting system for each and every student in your classroom.

Parent Call Worksheet

Student _____ Date _____

Parent _____ Phone Number _____

Parent called ____ Teacher called ____ Returning phone call ____

Reason for contact:

Points to cover:

1. Statement of concern:

2. Specific behavior that prompted call:

3. Steps I have taken to solve the problem:

4. Parental input:

5. Present solutions to problem (what I will do; what I need parent to do):

6. Inform parent that I will follow up with them:

Notes: Date of follow-up, etc.

Parent Conference Planning and Note Sheet

Student's Name _____ Time _____

Parent's Name _____ Date _____

1. Example of student's unique quality:

2. Past problems of the student to be updated at the conference:

3. Academic strengths of the student:

4. Academic weaknesses of the student that should be discussed:

5. Parent input on student's academic performance:

6. Academic goals for the student for the rest of the year:

7. Social strengths of the student:

8. Any weaknesses in the area of social development the student has:

9. Social development goals for the student for the rest of the year:

10. Parent input regarding student's social behavior:

11. Additional issues parent wishes to discuss:

CHAPTER 5

Organizing Homework Collection

Betsy Ann Wandishin

Casco, Maine

J ody always sits in the front of the room with a smile on her face, ready to start the day. Her pencil is sharp, and her math book is out, but something is missing: her homework. Of course, the teacher never figures out that her homework hasn't been handed in until she gets home at night and begins correcting her sets of papers. Mrs. Ryan's frustration increases as she fills in her grades for the assignment and realizes that she is missing not only Jody's assignment but those of four or five other students as well. She sighs and wishes once again that she had a system that allowed her to know in a more timely fashion which students had not handed in their homework for that day. When she returns to her classroom the next day, she will then have to take more precious time to hunt down and collect the late papers and sit down and correct them. Wouldn't it be nice to have a system of homework collection that completely removes the teacher from the process and makes students responsible for their own recording and organizing? The following strategies will help classroom teachers streamline their homework collection process and make students the organizers.

Helpful Tips

- Take a classroom attendance sheet or make your own spreadsheet with students' names for rows and blank columns across the top.
- Glue each sheet to a different-colored file folder, and write each subject heading at the top or bottom of the folder.
- Laminate the file folders and cut them out.
- Use overhead projector markers to write homework assignments on folders at the top of the columns.
- When students enter the classroom in the morning, they bring their homework to a designated table and sort it according to the subject folders. They put their homework in the folder and check their name in the appropriate column.
- If homework is not complete, students put a circle in the column and then fill out a "Homework Owed Slip."
- Homework slips must be signed by a parent and missing homework returned the next day.
- Folders can be rinsed off under the faucet at the end of each week.
- "Homework Honor Cards" can be used for students who occasionally miss an assignment. These cards have one "No Homework Pass" for each month of the school year. When circumstances prevent a student from completing an assignment, they may choose to get their card punched.
- I award students who complete all homework assignments in a week with a fair ticket. We keep the tickets in a bucket and each week I do a drawing. Winning students can choose from a variety of prizes in the classroom treasure chest.

Homework Owed Slip

Name _____ Date _____

Missing Assignment(s)	Original Due Date	Last Date Accepted

I understand that this work needs to be completed by the last date acceptable.

_____
Parent Signature

CHAPTER 6

The Harmonious Classroom

Sharon Andrews

Sioux Falls, South Dakota

A t the beginning of each new school year, teachers have hopes of acquiring complete harmony in their classrooms. Having courteous, kind, giving, and responsible students in our classes is a dream that all teachers share. We all search for the magic potion that will touch and reach all children. We all want to keep classroom disruptions to a minimum so that we can maximize instruction and learning. But soon, the dream of harmony fades as kids settle into the school year and return to their usual tactics of classroom disruption. What went wrong? How can we foster and maintain a harmonious classroom?

It is common practice to post school rules throughout the school building as a visible reminder to students as to the expected behavior in the school. Teachers also have classroom rules that are posted and reviewed on a regular basis. Some teachers write the rules themselves; others allow students to help compose the classroom rules together as a class. Children seem to have rules at every turn of the corner. There are playground rules, cafeteria rules, library rules, hallway rules, and classroom rules. These rules are usually written in imperative form such as, "Keep your hands and feet to yourself," or "Raise your hand before talking." When you think about it, rules such as these seem to be negatively stated and probably ignite the rebellious side in some children. Is there a way to retain expected behavior in our classrooms in a more positive way? Is there a way to have behavior expectations without having rules?

Most schools in the United States have always played a part in helping children build character while teaching basic virtues. After all, we all want kids to be honest when taking a test, responsible in turning in assignments, considerate when dealing with other people, and respectful when communicating with teachers and peers. So, instead of posting rules in my classroom, four years ago I researched and found five virtues (from William J. Bennett's book *The Book of Virtues*) that I felt were essential in creating a harmonious classroom. The virtues that I chose were honesty, respect, responsibility, caring, and giving.

When reviewing the rules that I had in my classroom, I discovered that most of my rules fit into one of Bennett's five virtue categories that I had chosen. For example, "Keep your hands and feet to yourself" and "Raise your hand before speaking" both fell under the virtue category of "respect." I then turned all of the virtues into the following classroom goals:

1. We are working toward being responsible.

2. We are working toward a caring classroom.

3. We are working toward being honest.

4. We are working toward a giving classroom.

5. We are working toward being respectful.

I later added two more goals of my own:

6. We are working toward a quiet classroom.

7. We are working toward a joyful classroom.

To me, having children work toward goals seemed like a more positive approach in managing classroom behavior, but would it work?

During the first week of school, I spent a lot of time defining the word "goal," talking about and discussing each one of the goals in detail and giving examples to make sure that everyone in the class understood. The students gathered into discussion groups and came up with examples of honesty, caring, respect, responsibility, and giving. The kids thought that it was cool that they would not have "rules." In addition, having goals instead of rules seemed to get everyone off to a positive start.

During the first few weeks of school, I had lunch with every child so that I could get to know them better. In today's world of single-parent families and families in which both parents work, a lot of children are hungry for one-on-one adult attention. This time investment really paid off. During our lunch together, we talked about family, likes and dislikes, and personal goals. Each student talked with me about behaviors in the past that he or she would like to eliminate or improve during the new school year.

After the lunch, students worked on their own personal goal sheet that they kept inside a notebook in their desk. On this sheet, students chose two goals that they would like to work on during the first nine weeks. Students were very tempted to write a vague or general goal such as, "I would like to become more responsible." I insisted that the children identified a specific goal such as, "I will turn my homework assignments in on time." After the student identified the goal, they wrote down an action plan such as, "I will do my homework immediately when I get home and put it in my backpack after I finish." Then students evaluated their progress in achieving their goals.

At the beginning of the year, the students evaluated their progress on their goals about once a week. Later, they evaluated themselves once every two weeks. If a goal was not being met, the student composed a different positive plan of action. This time I had a conference involving the student, the parent, and myself. Everyone involved in the conference came up with a joint contract. The contract contained sections that stated what the student would do, what the parent would do, and what the teacher would do. Everyone signed the contract and decided on a date to evaluate progress.

As the year progressed, I found that it was equally important to review the classroom goals and evaluate the class progress on a regular basis. For example, one of my classroom goals was working toward being a quiet classroom. I had two signals that told students that it was time to quiet down. One signal was flipping off the light and the other signal was raising my hand. At the beginning of the year, I gave one of the signals, patiently waited, and then noted the length of time that it took for everyone to respond. Then I made a comment like, "It took 20 seconds for the class to settle down. If we are working toward a quiet classroom, how long do you think it should take everyone to settle down? What do you think our goal should be?" The kids were much stricter on themselves than I was, so someone responded, "It should take us one second." Then I counteracted with, "How about five seconds?" Each day after that, the class evaluated themselves on how well they were doing at reaching the goal of five seconds. When they reached the goal, we celebrated.

I have been using goals instead of rules in my classroom for four years now. Establishing and maintaining a harmonious classroom has taken a lot of effort on my part, but I have found that it has been well worth it. Time spent at the beginning of the year to establish a sense of community and family has paid off in a monumental way. Maintaining the community climate throughout the year has been just as important, but it has often been difficult. As things become routine, children tend to become less eager to please than they were in the beginning of the year. Just as in real families, the more time people spend with one another, the more they tend to irritate one another. I have found that it has been important to be proactive in trying to anticipate problems before they have arisen.

Having regular class meetings to discuss and evaluate progress on classroom goals has kept the students focused. Occasional rewards or treats have motivated students as the school year continued. Learning and practicing conflict resolution strategies became increasingly essential as the year progressed. When conflicts arose, I always pointed out that members of a family do not always agree. As a natural part of maturation, everyone needs to learn how to handle conflicts in a caring and civilized way. I have found that children enjoy and appreciate learning how to deal with disagreements. After all, isn't this a skill with which many adults still struggle in their own relationships?

Helpful Tips

- Get to know your students early in the year. Have lunch with a few children at a time and get to know them personally. Discuss family, likes and dislikes, and talk about personal goals.
- Focus on building a cooperative atmosphere from the very first day of school. Talk about the classroom community and family. At the beginning of the year, kids are ready to please and are anxious for a fresh start. Capitalize on this!
- Be very specific with praise. Look for times when the class as a community is making progress toward the classroom goals. Identify the goal, the specific aspect of the goal that the class is doing well, and praise appropriately.
- Review the classroom goals on a regular basis and evaluate progress. Students should also individually review and evaluate progress on their personal goals.
- Discuss conflict resolution strategies on a regular basis. Have students role-play different situations in front of the class. This becomes particularly important as the year progresses and everyone begins to get on one another's nerves.
- Always be as positive as possible. Children are impulsive and will not always make good choices. Patiently talk with the child about how the situation could have been handled differently. A teacher's kind input and guidance could have a lasting effect on a child's life. Teachers can make a difference!

CHAPTER 7

Using Newsletters to Communicate With Families

Deborah Gordon

Phoenix, Arizona

G ood communication between parents and classroom teachers has become a critical component in today's classroom. There has been considerable research done on the benefits of developing a partnership between home and school. The most comprehensive series of research comes from Anne Henderson and Nancy Berla and their studies over the past twenty years. These are several of their findings:

- When parents are involved, students achieve more, regardless of socioeconomic status, ethnic and racial background, or the parents' education level.

- When parents are involved in their students' education, those students have higher grades and test scores, have better attendance, and complete homework more consistently.
- When parents are involved, students exhibit positive attitudes and behavior.

The National Parent and Teachers Association is so committed to this issue that it has published National Standards for Parent/Family Involvement Programs. Their goals are that "Every school will promote partnerships that will increase parental involvement and participation in promoting the social, emotional, and academic growth of children." Communication is their first standard, and it states, "Communication between home and school is regular, two-way, and meaningful."

A newsletter is the perfect way to communicate with the parents in your classroom. Newsletters can be weekly, biweekly, or monthly. The most effective ones are sent home each week providing parents with insight on weekly progress and thus helping them to support the learning at home. A newsletter, though, needs to be more than just a calendar of events. It should be purposeful, informative, and specific to each particular classroom. Several important elements should be included in every newsletter sent home:

- Details of the skills taught in each subject area that week (math, science, social studies, reading, and writing)
- State standards for the major concepts (math and language arts) worked on in class
- Dates for upcoming events
- Any changes in normal school routines (half day, no school, special events, etc.)

Several formats can be used when writing a newsletter. The most common formats are a newspaper approach, a template with boxes for each content area, and a narrative letter format. All of these work well to share information. Some teachers include a spot for students to write about what's happening in the classroom (this can take quite a bit of time, practice, and editing).

Newsletters can also be used for sharing ideas, suggestions, or strategies for ways that the learning can be extended at home. ("When reading with your child, practice ways to sound out an unknown word—please don't just tell them what the word is. We are developing strategies in class for figuring out unknown words. Ask your child about these strategies!")

In mathematics, a newsletter is a great way to show various strategies students are using to solve computation problems. ("We shared the various ways students are solving multiplication problems this week. Here are several of the strategies our class is using to solve this multiplication problem: 28×4.")

Distributive Strategy

(Distributing the Tens Place and the Ones Place)	*Doubling Strategy*	*Repeated Addition Strategy*
$20 \times 4 = 80$	$28 \times 2 = 56$	$28 + 28 = 56$
$8 \times 4 = 32$	$56 \times 2 = 112$	$28 + 28 = 56$
$80 + 32 = 112$	$(50 + 50) = 100$	112
	$6 + 6 = 12$	
	112	

Parents are curious about the changes they see in classroom practices. Homework looks different, and there may or may not be textbooks. Educating students has changed significantly over the past twenty-five years because of the ever-changing world we live in. The impact of technology, the changes in the job market, and changes in the global economy have created a world different from that in which most of today's parents grew up.

Newsletters are a wonderful tool that can bridge the gap between what once happened in classrooms and what is happening today. Newsletters can help parents understand, learn, support, and appreciate their child's education. Although writing a newsletter may take some extra effort and time, the substantial benefits of clear communication between the classroom and the home far outweigh the effort. Newsletters provide parents and teachers a connection to each other that will ultimately benefit all parties involved in the child's education.

Helpful Tips

- Write or type your newsletter so it is neat and legible.
- *Always* check for grammar and spelling errors.
- Be sure the information is accurate. Check dates and times.
- Make sure the content of your newsletter makes sense and that anyone who reads it can understand what you are saying.
- Distribute to parents and administrators and keep a copy for yourself.
- Keep the newsletter information focused on the classroom; this is not the place for your personal views or opinions.

CHAPTER 8

Building a Community of Learners

Zoma A. Barrett

Salem, Indiana

O n a crisp November afternoon inside my middle school classroom, twenty-two pairs of eyes are focused intently on Cathy, a sixth-grade student, who stands at the chalkboard demonstrating the process she used to arrive at the solution to a decimal division problem from last night's math homework. Only the sound of Cathy's voice and the scratch of the chalk against the board break the quiet in the classroom. As she completes her demonstration, Cathy turns to face her classmates, smiles broadly, extends her hand in which she holds the chalk, and says, "Jeffrey."

Head down and shoulders slightly drooping, Jeffrey slides slowly from his seat and makes his way toward Cathy. The other students watch quietly as he takes the chalk from Cathy's hand and writes the problem he is assigned to explain on the board. He stops, glances over his shoulder, and mutters, "I didn't get this one."

I say, "Let's try it together then." Jeffrey turns back toward the board and stares silently at the problem. I prompt, "What do we do first?" Jeffery remains silent for what seems to be an eternity, but the students and I wait patiently. I glance at their faces; they are watching Jeffrey attentively. Some seem to be willing him to say something.

Finally, the silence is broken when Jeffrey meekly says in a questioning tone, "Bring the decimal point up?"

I reply, "That's correct!" Jeffrey turns to look at me to make sure I said he was correct. I start to nod my head and notice that Cathy and several other students nod their heads encouragingly at Jeffrey, too. He turns back to the board and hesitantly makes his decimal point on the division bar in the correct place. He looks back toward his classmates and me for approval of his placement. More students nod in agreement now. I ask, "What do we do now?"

Jeffrey examines the problem again, and after several moments of silence, he turns toward the students and me and replies timidly, "Divide eight by four." This time there is no need for me to respond. Jeffrey's classmates are all nodding and many have broken into smiles. He straightens his shoulders, and his eyes brighten. He places the two in the correct place on the division bar and continues with his classmates offering their support and encouragement through each step in the explanation. When Jeffrey arrives at the solution to the problem, his classmates break into applause as he beams an appreciative smile at them. It is now his turn to select the student who will demonstrate the next problem. He extends his hand holding the chalk and says, "Michael."

At the end of the day, I find myself replaying this scene in my mind with a sense of satisfaction, and as I reflect on how we have arrived at this point, my mind drifts back to the first day of school when we began the journey to build a community of learners. I planned to begin the year with a getting-acquainted activity for my sixth-grade students. Before the children arrived, I arranged the desks, along with my chair, in a circle so that we could all see one another. As they entered the classroom, I observed my new charges. Some bounded into the room full of energy and flopped down in chairs, while others made their way cautiously through the door and found the nearest place to sit so that they wouldn't draw attention to themselves.

When time for class to begin arrived, I sat down in my chair and called roll, pausing to study each child's face so that I could commit it to memory. Then I shared with them the story of how I was named, followed by information about my family, my pets, and me, and I answered their questions about me and about school because this was their first year in the middle school. As the class period drew to a close, I gave the students their homework assignment: "Ask your parents how you were named and write down three things about yourself that you would like to share with the class." I explained that if, for some reason, they could not learn the story of how they were named or did not want to share it, they could share the things they wanted us to know.

Over the next two days in class, we all sat in our circle and listened as the children shared the stories of how they were named and other information about themselves. During this time, I could see the children making connections with one another. The following day, I told them that we were going to see how much they had learned about their classmates. I asked them to introduce one classmate and tell one thing that person shared. I told them that each person had to introduce someone different until all introductions had been made. This task was easy in the beginning but proved to be more challenging as it progressed. As they neared the end of the introductions, I told them that they could assist one another if needed, and several welcomed the help that was offered. This was the beginning of our community.

With introductions out of the way, it was time to present the next piece in building our community: developing rules. To lay the groundwork for developing our classroom rules, I gathered the children around me and read Dr. Suess's *Hooray for Diffendoofer Day!* I then led them in a discussion of what types of things would have to happen in our classroom if we were going to have an engaging classroom like the ones in Diffendoofer School. From this discussion, we developed a classroom behavior agreement, rules focused on observable physical behaviors; a classroom living agreement, rules governing how we interact with one another; and a classroom work agreement, rules focused on doing and submitting quality work. I formalized these by creating documents for each agreement with the rules listed on them, making classroom posters of the documents, and having the students sign their own personal copies of the agreements.

With the getting-acquainted and rule-developing activities completed, it was time to turn our attention to the next step in building our community: getting the parents involved. I wrote a letter to the parents detailing our classroom activities up to this point and outlining plans for the future. I included in the letter my teaching philosophy, the instructional strategies I planned to use, and my grading policy. I attached copies of the classroom agreements the students and I had developed to this letter. I also included a "Handle with Care" sheet that I asked the parents to complete and return. The "Handle with Care" sheet was designed to give the parents an opportunity to tell me about their children's strengths and weaknesses, to let me know about any concerns they had, and to open the door of communication for the rest of the year.

At this point, I realized that a week and a half of the school year had passed, and I had not yet begun mathematics instruction. I was not concerned, however, because I believe it is important to establish behavior management early in the year. With this in mind, I started the next phase in building our classroom community: establishing routines and procedures to add structure to our community. We practiced each of the routines so that they would know what to do and how to do it. I was then ready to move into beginning mathematics instruction; however, I knew that I needed to add a way to reinforce the desired behaviors we had discussed and practiced. Therefore, I introduced preferred activity time (PAT), which allowed the children, based on their behavior, the opportunity to earn or lose time toward participating in a math learning activity of their choice. During the period, if students followed routines and made positive behavior choices, they earned PAT; if they did not follow routines or made poor behavior choices, I deducted time. At the end of each week, I tallied the time earned and allowed the children to choose a math activity to do for that amount of time. It did not take long for the children to realize that they must work together to help everyone make positive choices so that they would be successful in attaining the maximum amount of PAT. This was a valuable piece for the development of our community.

With all the rules, routines, and procedures established, I turned my attention to adding the supported learning component to our community. I began by having the children work in cooperative learning groups to complete a problem-solving activity in which they were not allowed to speak or take things from members in their group, but they were allowed to give things to one another or acquire assistance from others outside their group. Not only did the children gain insight into behaviors that helped their group work more successfully, but they also learned the importance of supporting one another within their small groups and within the larger group to solve problems.

I spent the next two weeks doing math review work and more group problem-solving activities as I reinforced the positive behaviors that were growing within our classroom community. Confident that the children were ready for the next step in building our community, I introduced Socratic seminars. Through these seminars, the students learned to state and support their thoughts, to disagree respectfully with one another, and to collaborate to arrive at a solution to a problem.

Although I was pleased with the progress of our community building, I knew I had one more important piece that had to be put into place for each student to become a productive part of our community of learners. That piece was the ability to risk being incorrect in front of their peers. In Socratic seminars, they had the opportunity to pass, which protected them from this risk. Although this protection can be beneficial, especially at the middle school age, it can also encourage students who have not experienced academic success to be more passive. I did not want this; therefore, I started having the students put assigned problems on the chalkboard and explain the process they used to arrive at their solutions. I knew this would require the students to risk being incorrect in front of their peers, which is extremely difficult for them, and thus I encouraged them to think of mistakes as opportunities to learn. Soon, students were saying, "Mistakes are opportunities to learn," and assisting one another in correcting the problems. We had finally become a working, productive community of learners.

This is not to say that everything was, or is, perfect in my classroom. There were, and still are, trials for students, just as I described earlier with Jeffrey, but there also exists a desire to support and encourage one another with the classroom community we have built. In the scene played out that November day in my classroom, Cathy realized that Jeffrey was struggling to do decimal division and that he wasn't feeling good about himself. She extended her hand and selected Jeffrey so that the students would have a chance to support and encourage him in his attempt to master this concept!

Helpful Tips

- Invest time at the beginning of the year to teach behavior expectations in your classroom.
- Spend time getting to know the students and their life stories; it helps in making decisions on how to handle poor behavior choices.
- Write positive notes home to parents so that they can celebrate their children's accomplishments; this keeps communication open and makes difficult discussions about behavior easier to have.
- Make school a place the students want to be; if you make learning exciting and interesting, most will want to be there.

CHAPTER 9

Corresponding With Parents

Mary Eby

Woodbine, Iowa

P arents want and need to know what is being taught to their children in the classroom. More and more parents are taking an active role in educating their children. It is essential that the classroom teacher provide parents with current and accurate information.

I use a weekly newsletter that goes home with the student in a folder on Friday. I accumulate all of the paper-and-pencil work, worksheets, tests, center work, copies of journal entries, and so on, throughout the week. On Friday, all of the student's work, along with the school newsletter, spelling list, and classroom newsletter, goes home in a two-pocket folder with the child. A parent or guardian then signs the newsletter, and it is returned with the folder on Monday.

The newsletter is designed with bubbles for the information rather than in a letter form. There are bubbles for four academic subjects that are titled "What We Have Learned This Week." I use a bubble for language arts, math, social studies, and science. There is also a section titled

"Special Activities." I use it for any assemblies that we have had, special guests to our room, special activities in music, art, and so on.

There is a bubble for "Things to Work On at Home." I use this bubble to make a list of specific concepts that we have worked on during the week that need extra practice or reinforcement at home, such as counting money, telling time, regrouping in addition or subtraction, and using capital letters and correct ending marks at the ends of sentences. I have a bubble for "Reminders." This bubble reminds parents to send warm hats and mittens, that we have a spelling pretest every Wednesday, and of conferences, school dates, school parties, and other important dates to remember. Often this section is a repeat of the school newsletter, but I have found that parents read the classroom newsletter more thoroughly than the school newsletter.

Something new that I have added in the past year is a behavior chart on the back of the newsletter. I didn't realize the impact this short, simple chart would have on the parents. They read it faithfully every week and comment to me. This chart has opened up the channels of communication between parents and teacher more than anything else I have done. The kids in my class also look at their chart each week before they take home their folder. They have started to become self-disciplinarians. They understand which behavior needs to be changed and at which behaviors they are doing well. I also have an area for teacher comments and an area for parent comments. If there is an area of concern or if something has happened during the week that the parents need to be aware of, this is where I can elaborate. I also use this area for praise.

All too often, teachers send home negative comments and tend to forget the positive. Children of all ages need praise and positive feedback. Parents often write back to me. They relay what they have been working on with their children at home, academic areas that they see need more work, concerns they have for their children, and often just a thank-you for making them aware of a concern that I have or a thank-you for praising their child.

If the newsletter does not return on Monday, I wait one more day, then I give the parents a quick phone call reminding them to return the signed newsletter. After a couple of phone calls, there is no longer a problem of returning the newsletter. Because of the informal format of the newsletter, even noninvolved parents find time to look at it.

When filling the take-home folders, I always put the spelling list, school newsletter, and the classroom newsletter on a separate side of the two-pocket folder. The classroom newsletter goes on the top. All of the academic work is put on the opposite side of the folder. I try to put all language arts papers together, all math papers together, and so on. The parents can then see the sequential progression of what we have worked on during the week. I find the weekly newsletter and take-home folder a valuable tool for my classroom management.

CHAPTER 10

Classroom Posters

"Welcome to My Ball Park" and
"The Scoring Guide to Whining"

Cliff B. Barrineau

Columbia, South Carolina

B efore I start, let me explain that I was a vice principal in charge of discipline for a high school other than the one in which I now teach for three years back in the early 1990s. During that time, I was responsible for expulsion cases and any student arrests at the school. Through that experience, I learned that the best tools for classroom management involve rarely reacting with anger, being as fair and consistent as possible, always making choices that are *in the best interest of children,* and having a good sense of humor. Although there will be school and district guidelines we all follow in our classes, these can be attended to with a sense of humor. For example, I have two posters on the wall of my classroom that demonstrate how I try to use humor in my approach to rules and reactions to "less than desirable responses from students" (I received these from fellow educators a few years ago and am not sure of their origin). One poster reads as follows:

38

Welcome to Dr. Barrineau's class,
This is my ballpark, We use my ball,
I am the umpire, I make the rules,
I own this team, Therefore, I win.
Thanks for playing!

I believe there is a lot of truth in these statements and have used this effectively for the past six years. I also have a poster in my room that is a "scoring guide for whining," which ranks whines from one to six. A rank of one is interpreted as no one in the room heard the whine, so no one cared. A rank of six is interpreted as most of the students in the room heard the whine and gave it some thought, as well as the teacher, but it still did not accomplish its goal.

I must also add that by having these in my classroom, I am not "out to get the students," but that I do expect them to behave as young ladies and gentlemen and be responsible for their behavior. Although I infuse humor into the messages from these posters, I do not provide students the option of blaming anyone but themselves for their behaviors and want to teach them that whining is useless.

One example of how I use these in my class, along with student reactions and responses, is evident by the following anecdote:

Last week in my class, one young lady asked me about their next unit test. I explained that the test would be given as planned in the unit of study guide they received the week before. She questioned whether I knew that I had planned a test just a few days after the Super Bowl (three days to be exact) and why would I do that. I did not get angry or raise my voice, but smiled, pointed to one poster and explained that her response (whine) could possibly get a ranking of three. I then started reading from the other poster, "This is my ballpark. We use my ball. I am the umpire. I make the rules." Before I got to the last sentence and started reading the whining guide, she said, "Okay, okay, I will plan to study ahead!" I said, "Thanks for playing!"

The class in which this took place is an honors algebra II class, which is required to take district-level assessments at the end of each grading period. Therefore, covering material in a timely fashion is essential. That is why I chose to respond as I did.

Another incident, more severe than this first one, dealt with students in a nonhonors class.

One young lady announced aloud during the last five minutes of class that her birthday was in one week and that she expected presents. A second young lady in the class responded just loud enough to be heard, "Why don't you shut the hell up?" I could have gotten very angry but quickly decided that my anger on top of the second young lady's response was probably not going to help resolve the matters at hand. Rather, I calmly responded to the first young lady, "We will be happy to give you our presence (not presents) on your birthday!" I then turned to the second young lady and told her I expected to see her after class and that I would not allow young ladies to use that type of language in my ballpark. After class I handed her a sheet with the sentence, "I understand that saying 'shut the hell up' during class is not appropriate or acceptable, and I promise to never use that type of language again as it is not becoming of a young lady." I asked her to write the sentence one hundred times in her own handwriting before the start of the next class (two days after this incident) and have her mother sign the sentences.

When she started to explain that she would not do this because of all she had to do, I walked over to the whine poster and told her that her response was either a one or a two on the ranking guide but definitely not higher. I also explained that if she made the choice not to do the sentences, I would first phone her parents to explain the situation, her choice, and then explain to the school disciplinarian that I had tried to deal with her behavior in a way I though appropriate but that she would not cooperate. I also explained to her that this was how I dealt with behaviors in my class because (as I pointed to the poster), "This is my ballpark. We use my ball. I am the umpire. I make the rules." She brought the sentences to me with her parents' signature the next class.

Although this plan may not work with all students in all situations, I have been blessed in that it has worked well in my classes with my students. I have also been blessed to have written less than five disciplinary referrals in the past eight years; I have tried to use school disciplinarians as a very last resort. I believe this type of plan will cover most behaviors that teachers deal with most often.

CHAPTER 11

Classroom Management and Finding Success in Your AP Spanish Program

Jesus "Jesse" Bernal

Garden City, Kansas

You should have a vision and establish a plan that includes methods, strategies, and innovative ideas, which will increase your students' success in learning and scores on the Spanish Advanced Placement (AP) Test.

 Vision

I remember showing the video *Stand and Deliver* in my classes. Jaime Escalante challenged his students to believe in themselves and their potential to succeed in calculus class. I felt this film would help motivate my students to stay in school and do well in other classes. Little did I know that this would have a bigger impact on me and ignite a fire and love for teaching. That was the start of my vision. I began to think, "What can I do to improve learning outcomes and challenge my students in our Spanish classes?"

Plan

I needed to inform myself on how to establish an AP program. I started by visiting with colleagues who had AP programs already in place at our high school. I gained support from the administration, and they decided to send me to an AP Spanish Summer Institute at the University of Northern Colorado. My next step was to write up the requirements and guidelines for our AP/honors class. I worked closely with foreign language staff and the counseling department. Finally, we were ready to submit to the curriculum council. We offered our first AP/honors class in the 1993–1994 school year. Our Spanish department worked on specific objectives that would enhance learning outcomes for each level. We also visited with parents during parent-teacher conferences to gain support.

Methods

Flexibility in our methods of teaching must be our strength. Our school is on a block schedule, so in my daily lesson plans, I need to use different methods of teaching and activities to keep my students on task. Grammar and an oral communicative approach is a big part of my teaching style. I also find time to use cooperative learning. Develop your own teaching style, and remember to involve your students in choosing and creating activities that will help them with the learning process. AP Spanish classes can be fun.

Strategies

We need to make our students feel the connection to why this is important for them. Provide open discussions on the importance of having bilingual skills and how this can improve career opportunities.

The Research and Education Association puts out *The Best Text Preparation for the Advanced Placement Examination Book,* which provides three full-length practice exams. I feel that this has helped my students better prepare themselves. I would also like to share some strategies that I use.

Our school provides a daily forty-minute Opportunity Period. Students can use this for study time or travel to other classes to make up missed assignments. My AP/honors students can earn extra credit by working with the Chapter 2 AP Spanish Review from this book.

The book offers a total of seventeen drill sections on grammar. Because of low budgets and lack of practice books, I tried something new this year that has worked well. I had students choose teams, three students for each team. I used this section to show students that learning can be fun and that they can learn from one another. Students in each team can discuss and choose the correct answer for questions. After each drill, we verify our answers by using the detailed Explanations of Answers Section. Teams tally their correct answers, and students compete for prizes. At the end of all drills, we choose the top three teams. The community can get involved by providing coupons for pizza, movie tickets, and other items. Students also get participation points for their class grade. Those absent during these activities can make up assignments during Opportunity Period.

The Practice Test Section is used to improve individual performance. I help students with test-taking strategies. I applied for a grant and used that money to purchase recorders and cassettes so that students can practice the picture series and directed-response part of the test. I use essay topics to evaluate organization, grammatical accuracy, and use of vocabulary. Students are encouraged to use the wheel process, or other methods, to organize their thoughts and ideas.

Helpful Tips

Establish a close network of communication with other AP Spanish instructors in your state. I have learned and shared many ideas by attending AP conferences and joining organizations such as the Kansas Foreign Language Association and the American

Association of Teachers of Spanish and Portuguese. Two years ago we started up a local chapter of the Spanish National Honor Society at our school.

Have your AP/honors students use their language skills by getting involved in school and community service. Our students translate articles and provide a bilingual section in our school newspaper, *The Sugar Beat*. They also volunteer to help serve as translators during election time. Another project we do is to have them translate or create children's books. These bilingual books are used when the students visit elementary schools during scheduled reading times. Our AP/honors class also takes the National Spanish Exam the first week of March. I have ordered tests from the past so students can be familiar with the format of test questions and get practice time.

We started with a small AP class and are happy to say that our numbers reached forty-five students last year. With this success, we have also met new challenges. Most of our students come from low-income families and would not consider taking a test they would also have to pay for. To meet this challenge, we do two major fundraisers during the year. In February, we have an enchilada sale. In April, we do a garage sale, and students can earn extra credit by bringing items to sell. Our high school staff is very supportive of this project. Helping students raise funds helps teach responsibility and builds a special bond among classmates.

CHAPTER 12

One Teacher's Journey to the Classroom of the Future

Carrie Jane Carpenter

Redmond, Oregon

Does imagining the technology-laden classroom of the future put fear into your heart, or a lilt in your step? Most likely it depends on your experiences with technology. If you have failed miserably in front of a class of thirty-four "active" seventh graders as I did in my first attempt to use technology as a teaching tool, most likely your interest in technology has been snuffed out like a wavering candle in a damp and drafty room.

Some work of educational magic must certainly have occurred to take me from being a tech failure to being a Master Teacher for the Intel Teach to the Future Program and an Oregon Teacher of the Year. I have to give that credit to our district tech support people and my administrator. They believed me when I said I wanted to be a leader in my school in the area of technology. They provided me with support when I floundered. And they didn't believe me each time I got frustrated and said that I didn't want to do "IT" (information technology) anymore.

I started as many teachers do; I took some summer classes to learn how to use technology. PowerPoint was my tool of choice. The class was so frustrating. I felt so stupid. But then, as I got the hang of it, I discovered that IT was fun! IT made my presentations look professional. I knew that a picture was worth a thousand words, so I used pictures to show the passion that I had for language arts. I could take my students thousands of miles away to the New Globe Theatre and hundreds of years back in time by projecting Shakespeare's words on the big screen for all to absorb. I couldn't wait to share my creations with my new students. I was going to look like such a capable teacher. Technology gave me power!

At least I thought I had power until the first day of school that fall. The mammoth projector hummed benignly but refused to project my PowerPoint work of art onto the dark screen. I was mortified. It didn't help that I had bragged myself up just a little to my students. I may have even insinuated that I had "mastered" PowerPoint, and it was now at my every beck and call.

My students were actually very patient. Several offered to help me, but I felt like a small, furry rabbit surrounded by a pack of hungry, drooling coyotes. No way would I allow these potentially judgmental— but knowledgeable—people prove beyond a shadow of a doubt that I, the teacher, was a failure.

Quickly, I swept technology under the rug. The huge lump in the carpet was easy to ignore, because I just went back to teaching along the friendly path that I had always used. IT didn't trip me up until I met with my administrator to discuss my yearly goals. I had successfully, if not guiltily, repressed my August excitement for technology. I had conveniently forgotten the goal that I had written with my very hand just a few weeks earlier.

Donna, my administrator, was eager to hear about the goal I had to lead our *entire* staff into the future of technology. I began to believe that I might actually die before I could get out the door of her upbeat office. And when an autopsy was performed, I would make headlines as the first person to succumb to the seduction of misled educational enthusiasm.

I didn't want to lie to Donna, so I omitted a few details, and I hemmed and hawed. I smiled brightly as I promised to look at software and maybe attend a conference. After all, I had a good seven months to find some other goal to distract her from the false lure of technology in the classroom. The problem was that she wholeheartedly believed in me. She didn't know that I was really just a coward in teachers' clothing.

A few weeks later, our lab person, Leasa, brought me a star-spangled box titled "Inspiration." It was new software that Donna wanted me to try. My heart beat wildly. My hands began to sweat. I had never loaded software. Miraculously, it almost loaded itself. A screen appeared with a neat blue oval in the center. Hmmmm, what should I try to map? Three hours flew by like three minutes. Finally, I sat back and looked at the mind map I had created using Inspiration software. The map illustrated everything I believed about education. At the top, I had written in an oval, "My students deserve the best teacher I can be." Toward the middle was an oval that said, "I must send my students into the world with the skills they need to be successful." Arrows jetted from that oval to list the skills of "reading," "writing," "speaking," "collaborating," "critical thinking," and "technology."

As I reflected on my work, a quote spiraled in and out of my thoughts. Albert Einstein said that "Teaching should be such that what is offered is perceived as a valuable gift." I had been given an incredible gift, a gift that solidified my teaching philosophy and my purpose in just a matter of hours. By the way, the mapping of personal educational philosophy is an activity that I believe all teachers should undertake and revisit periodically, especially in those times when we lose sight of the importance of the work we do in the world today.

I truly felt that I must also give my students this gift of technology, especially my students from disadvantaged homes who would be far behind their wealthy peers if computers were not provided at school. How could I live with myself if I did not use my beliefs about teaching to guide the development of my curriculum? If I was a person of character who was honorable enough to deserve the title of "teacher," I must be unflagging in my zeal for learning. I must take risks and push myself to learn as well.

Not much later, I learned that I had been duped. Leasa came back to see how I liked Inspiration. Of course, I wanted her to see how successful I had been, so I dove into deep water and shared my mind map with her. She was thrilled. Little did I know, but she was about to trap me into giving up a three-day weekend! Before I knew what hit me, I was attending the Instructional Technology Strategies Conference in Eugene, Oregon, over the Martin Luther King Jr. holiday of 2000. I listened to dynamic, impassioned speakers who showed me the classroom of the future. It was filled with interaction and choice, spontaneity and limitlessness. In the team sessions, tech people from our district surrounded me. They wanted a teacher's view on instructional technology. I spoke, and they listened. I talked about my failure. They offered me onsite tech support. My head was reeling, but never have I been more energized about my profession.

At the conference, I met Justin, a nice young man from our district. I would soon find out that he had the patience of a saint and the ideals of a visionary. He was the instructional technology specialist for our schools. He offered to come to my class and help me use technology. Not only did he help me take my current unit and enhance it with technology, but also part of his job was to help me teach my students to use technology. The offer sounded too good to be true. I might add that this model of mentoring is one that has been successfully duplicated and that I also recommend.

A wind of change blew into my classroom. A buzz of excitement filled the room each day as we learned technology and poetry, hand in hand. When something didn't work, Justin fixed it. When I didn't know how to teach a tech skill, he effortlessly stepped into my teaching shoes. One Friday when I was exhausted and I even told him I never wanted to use IT again, he simply shrugged and said he would talk to me on Monday. Together we made a great team, and it is a partnership that I am happy to say is in its fifth year.

So that Monday came and my kids began their poetry PowerPoint presentations. Justin and I sat in the back of my room. We laughed, we held back tears, and we applauded at the conclusion of each presentation. I scored my students using our state scoring guide for communication. When the last student left the room, he turned to me and asked a simple, but profound question: "Did you have results like this when you taught without technology?" I felt a wave of shock overtake me as I realized the dynamics that had just taken place in that room. I looked at my grade sheet. All but one seventh grader had met the eighth-grade benchmark for communication, and that one student added to her presentation and met the benchmark later that week. Never had I seen so much enthusiasm for learning. Never had I experienced the power of students teaching students. Never could I return to my old way of teaching.

Both Robert Frost and I have found that "as way leads on to way," we look back with a sigh. As devoted as I am to instructional technology, I know that it is a difficult road to travel. Hardware is expensive when we lack money in schools. We feel lucky if the hardware lasts three years. Ultimately, should we purchase hardware instead of reducing class sizes? Instructional technology training is marching into an uncharted wilderness. It often does not teach teachers how to lead students from knowledge to application to critical thinking, or to troubleshoot for temperamental hardware. Technological bells and whistles take the place of authentic curriculum planning. Expensive software is seen as a quick fix and then discarded as just an illusion produced by smoke and mirrors. Finally, the Internet, the door to vast amounts of knowledge, is also home to quacks and dangerous criminals. Is it really worth all the trouble?

I have one more story to tell. It is about three students, a teacher, a superintendent, and a school board director. The superintendent and the director were in the building for a visit. The teacher, who was often referred to as a "gutsy broad" by her father, made a split-second decision to invite the superintendent and the director into her room to watch students use technology. After the students left, they discussed the learning that had been so apparent in that room. The teacher asked them to remember the last three students they had watched. She asked if they could identify which student was labeled TAG (talented and gifted), which student was labeled LD (learning disabled), and which student was just a typical eighth grader. They could not distinguish between the abilities or skill levels of the three students.

Of course, that teacher was I. Thinking back, I wonder who in their right mind would invite the superintendent and a director unannounced into a middle school classroom? Was I crazy? Or was I and do I continue to be convinced that dedicated teachers, sound teaching practices, and technology can level the playing field for all students? The choice is yours; I've made mine.

Helpful Tips

- Remember, the relationship between the teacher and the students is the most important element of a successful classroom.
- Learning takes place in an environment of safe risk taking.
- Students are great teachers, so it's okay if they know more about the technology than you do. Give them the opportunity to shine in front of their peers.
- Technology is a tool that teachers should choose only when it is the best tool for the curriculum goals.
- When implementing a technology tool for the first time, choose a unit or lesson with which you already feel comfortable and enhance it with technology. It is difficult to master a new unit and new technology at the same time.
- Look for tech support people and tech-savvy teachers to help you. Don't be afraid to ask for help.
- Be nice to tech support people. They don't sabotage equipment just to make your life miserable! Being part of a team and learning to laugh at your mistakes are fun.
- Talk up technology and involve your community. They often magically come up with computers, scanners, printers, and handhelds for you.
- Learning is fun and makes you young, so become a student whenever possible.
- Professional development doesn't have to be expensive; arrange for a tech-savvy teacher to show a group how he or she uses IT.
- Hold on to your hat! It is a wild ride that you just may learn to love!

CHAPTER 13

Learning Through Love

Randy Heite

Evanston, Illinois

The most effective form of classroom management that I use for behavior modification was not learned in any of my college teaching courses. I didn't pick it up at any of the several teaching conferences I attended early in my career. I was not enlightened at an inservice day, or edified at one of our ninety-minute staff meetings. It was something I always had with me, just one of those things teachers never talk about. Come to think of it, it was a lesson one of my students taught me during my second year of teaching.

That second year had started with great enthusiasm and excitement. I made it through my first year of teaching kindergarten, and I had learned many of the do's and don'ts of teaching five-year-old children. I'll never forget Thomas standing with his head sticking out of the bathroom door shouting across the classroom, "I don't have ants in my pants, Mr. Heite!" He actually checked his pants after I had used an expression to describe the "ants in his pants" behavior during our story time. A lesson learned that first year? Kindergarten children will take things you say literally. You say it, and they'll believe it.

During my second year of teaching, I had one of those children that just seemed to know how to disrupt the classroom environment, no matter what you did to manage their behavior. You know whom I'm describing; we've all had one or two of them and their names are forever etched in your memory. That year, this student was Ronald.

On this particular day, Ronald was having difficulties once again, hitting his classmates and not being respectful to his teacher. As part of the routine, I told him he would be having a time-out with me on the bench during our recess time so we could talk about his behavior. My protocol was easy. I would sit next to him. I would ask him to tell me what he did wrong. And finally, I would proceed by reteaching the proper behavior that I expected from all of the children in Room 101. It wasn't very effective, but I had it down to a science—remember, this was only my second class ever.

Anyway, I'll never forget the day. It was beautiful. Not a cloud in the sky, and the air had that crisp, cool, fall feel to it. You know the feeling, like the bottom crisper drawer of your refrigerator. Well, the class was thrilled to be outside, and the children's happy roar echoed as we exited the playground door. We were all excited, except Ronald. He sat in his typical style with his arms crossed, eyebrows furrowed, and his cheeks full of air. He would often huff and puff to let me know he was angry in case I couldn't put the other clues together. But this day was different. When I walked to the bench and sat beside him, he was quiet.

After a minute or so of watching his classmates play, Ronald turned to me and shouted, "Mr. Heite, I hate you!" I could feel his eyes looking at the side of my head as I sat there thinking to myself, "Wow, he's angry!" No one had ever said that to me before, and I had no clue how a teacher should respond to that kind of remark. He stumped me, but after a brief moment, I turned to him, looked into his angry little face, and said, "Ronald, I love you and I care about you. You're here on the bench with me because I do not want you to grow up thinking it's okay to hurt people." I went on blabbering about school rules, classroom rules, and my expectations because that's how I changed behavior. When I was done with my chatter, thinking he had heard every word, Ronald looked up at me and asked in a dumbfounded way, "You love me?" I let out a chuckle. He smiled, and I proceeded to let him know how talented, wonderful, and unique he was. He was embarrassed, but he listened. His face lit up when I began naming the specific kind and caring things he did for me and his classmates as well as all the wonderful ways he makes positive contributions to our classroom community.

Recess was over, he hugged me, and he skipped off to join his classmates to stand in line. From that day forward, Ronald was a different child. His behavior changed, and he loved coming to school. He would actually tell his classmates and me that he loved us. And I don't recall his ever having a time-out after that, although he would often sit with me on the bench to talk, tell stories, and laugh.

The lesson Ronald taught me that day was how important it is to communicate your care and concern with your students. In his case, he needed to hear that he was loved. I learned the importance of creating a safe nurturing environment. And because of Ronald, I manage to create a classroom community of people who tell one another they're loved. The kind of love that we have for our fellow brothers and sisters. The kind of love that helps those in need. The kind of love that sees the potential in others. The kind of love that loves us when we blow it. The kind of love that encourages. The kind of love my mom was talking about when she used to say, "You don't have to like everyone, but you do have to love them."

We've all had teachers who loved us. Teachers who used a loving approach to reach out to us during our worst of times. And like Ronald, I bet that's what encouraged you to do your best. To be respectful. To be caring. To become a learner. When I tell friends and colleagues the lesson Ronald taught me that day, they often tell me their own stories about the teachers who loved them. I know you're out there. I've heard all about you when Mat shared the story of his eighth-grade German teacher, Frau Bartz, in LaGrange, Illinois. She gave him the extra support when his confidence wasn't so great. Ali told me about her kindergarten teacher, Ms. Davidson in Wapakoneta, Ohio. When Ali's mother passed away, Ms. Davidson would often baby-sit and bring her trusty accordion along. Kevin told me about his first- and second-grade teacher, Ms. Brown, in Buffalo, New York. He felt safe, cared for, and loved in the classroom environment she created. And Colm, he recalled stories of Ms. Drew in Tipperary, Ireland. In her class, students felt love and were encouraged to be creative, expressive, and themselves.

When you look back on your educational experience and think about those teachers who had the best classroom management approaches, who do you think of? Do you remember the ones who loved you?

CHAPTER 14

Rules! Rules! Rules!

Chris Laster

Smyrna, Georgia

R ules! Rules! Rules! It seems that in these days of zero-tolerance that there is a hard-and-fast rule to cover everything. "Playing cowboy? I don't think so! That pointed 'bang bang' finger is a weapon, mister! Five days out of school. Let's call Mom after we file the police report!"

Rare is the school system in this country that doesn't instill terror with a zero-tolerance policy that winds and twists through tens, even hundreds, of pages filled with small print and codes, rules, articles, sections and subsections, paragraphs, and lines of legal terms and definitions that make even the most educated people scratch their heads. And these are written for ten-year-olds! Does your classroom really need to pile a few more rules onto the heap?

The United States was essentially built on the Constitution and a set of ten succinctly stated rights that we all share, the Bill of Rights. The idea was simple, and even though it isn't perfect, it has thrived and proliferated around the world for more than two hundred years. I can think of no model more successful to emulate in the classroom.

My classroom operates on our own Bill of Rights and one rule (known as "The Rule"), both of which apply equally to students, teachers, and visitors. My classroom Bill of Rights and The Rule are as follows:

- You have the right to learn.
- You have the right to be safe.
- You have the right to be helped.
- You have the right to be treated respectfully.
- You have the right to be heard.
- The Rule: "Use good judgment and common sense."

What about consequences? Many teachers (including myself once upon a time) have a list of rules and consequences posted on the wall. I know elementary school teachers who post twenty rules or more! The rules always include a system of clips, checks, marks, or smiley faces that move up and down, left or right, throughout the day or week depending on individual student behavior. If your mark makes its way past a predetermined point, then you are meted out some low-level consequence like the dreaded ten minutes of lost recess. As the mark climbs, so does the severity of the consequences. Usually "Phone Call Home" followed by "Go to the Office" top the list. This is a nice system of accounting, but I'd rather be teaching!

Do I have consequences in my classroom? Absolutely, but they are not clearly delineated in systematic fashion. We are dealing with children, not computers that require us to bubble in A, B, C, or D. In considering consequences, I, too, follow The Rule: I use good judgment and common sense. I am not beholden to a wall chart to take away ten minutes of recess, although that is an option. I now have the freedom to apply a consequence that is both appropriate and directly applicable to the situation. How liberating to people who have devoted their lives to teaching children! Most important, I am free to talk with a student or the class as a whole so that they understand how their behavior lacked good judgment and what other choices might have been made—in short, how did your actions infringe on the rights of others, and how and why do you prevent that from happening in the future?

Do some students come to school lacking good judgment and common sense? Without a doubt they do, but walking into a classroom with a rigid system of rules and consequences does not automatically instill in them a personal value system guided by good judgment and common sense. It *will* teach them behaviors of self-preservation such as how to lie or be sneaky to avoid being caught. It will *not* teach them to take ownership of their actions.

Does one rule and a classroom Bill of Rights translate to spending less time dealing with issues of classroom discipline and management? No, at least not at first! It means that every incident becomes a learning experience. In truth, during the early part of the school year, a *lot* of time is spent each day working out disciplinary issues ranging from an occasional fight to lots of "He's messing with me." Well before midyear, however, our students have grown and matured to the point that our learning is interrupted more by the noise coming from the teachers' lounge next door than from any student disruptions. Moreover, by then I'm usually surrounded by individuals who I feel I can trust and who respect one another. When we reach that point, the academic possibilities are limitless. If we want our kids to engage in meaningful educational experiences that will require them to cooperate and apply higher-level thinking skills, then they must first develop and nurture a set of core values and principles. Stringent rules and consequences work well as crowd-control measures to help you survive the school year, but sooner or later, these young people will become adults in the same world in which we all live.

This is not touchy-feely nonsense; it is teaching! It means that I no longer have the option of hiding behind the curtain of "I'm sorry, but that's the policy!" It means that sometimes I have to make hard decisions—painful decisions—for which I am solely responsible, decisions I must sometimes explain to a parent or administrator. It means that I must be a role model who displays the same qualities that I expect of my students.

As teachers, we often dream of the "teachable moment," that moment in time when circumstances seem to conspire spontaneously to provide a few minutes of pure learning joy between ourselves and our students. It shouldn't be a dream. The students who we teach and love are, like us, little bundles of joy and imperfection. And buried in all of those moments of imperfection, those moments that make us groan and fuss and roll our eyes, is a teachable moment. It is right there in front of us, every single day! Over the course of eleven years in the classroom at a high-risk school, I have handed out just about every type of consequence imaginable, from a disappointing shake of the head to recommending expulsion from school. Through it all, I always try to make it a teachable moment. I want that individual to take away something positive from the experience that will make him or her a better, stronger person who is better equipped to succeed in life.

Helpful Tips

- Don't get in a rush to charge through curriculum during the first few weeks of school. Just plan on having many "teachable moments" throughout the day. It will save you enormous amounts of time in the future and enable you to do much more meaningful work later if you focus on establishing routines and expectations early.
- Spend a lot of time on the first days of school discussing and having the students role-play various situations. This provides them with a concrete frame of reference on how good judgment and common sense can be exercised. You can even make videotapes to show in later years for review and critique.
- When you see a student demonstrating good judgment in a situation in which he or she might have easily done otherwise, stop and point it out. The praise certainly doesn't hurt, and it's a real-life moment being modeled successfully in the real world right in front of you.
- When you fail to exercise either good judgment or common sense (and it will happen), be mature enough to accept responsibility for it. Your credibility factor will soar! I even allow students to use their "good judgment and common sense" to dole out an appropriate consequence for me.
- As much as possible, try to make every situation that requires a teacher intervention a learning experience for the entire class. Using your "good judgment" about how those directly involved might feel or be affected, you may want to share some of the details about what happened and have an impromptu classroom discussion about how and why better judgment could have been applied and how someone's rights were compromised. If you're

not sure how a student feels about sharing it with the class, ask them! Clearly, some situations (sexual harassment, for example) would demand that you keep it totally private.

- Remember that you are a "teacher." What an honor and a privilege that the purpose of your existence within a school is to teach. That is not limited to the three Rs. You must also teach kids how to become responsible individuals in every facet of their lives.

- When discussing a disciplinary issue with students, ask them what they feel would be an appropriate consequence. They will almost always come up with some punishment that is far more horrific than the offense. In their mind, this helps to put your final decision in perspective.

- I teach with a woman named Jean who has taught for more than thirty years and is probably more qualified than me to contribute to this book. One day after school, Jean was in the hallway listening to a teacher's harrowed and frustrated pleas about a student's repeated irresponsible behavior.

"What do I do with him? I've tried everything and he still keeps on and on! What am I supposed to do?"

Jean replied, "You love him."

In the end, I can think of no better advice than that!

CHAPTER 15

Making Connections

Effective Telephone Communications

John P. Pieper

Oshkosh, Wisconsin

"**M**r. Pieper, I don't understand question number four on my math assignment. Could you explain it to me?" Sally asked. After a short conversation, the question had been answered, and Sally was able to complete the rest of her assignment.

Teachers face this type of scenario many times each and every day. What made this situation different was that the student had called the teacher at home long after the school day had ended.

Maintaining good lines of communication with the students, parents, and staff is an essential element for creating a successful classroom. Carefully implemented communication techniques can facilitate learning, promote positive relations with parents, and provide viable data.

On the first day of school, the students are encouraged to write my home phone number down in their daily planners. Most of the students are shocked that a teacher would actually do that.

I carefully explain to the students that they are welcome to call me at home during the early evening hours, and even on weekends, if they have any questions about homework. A letter to the parents is also sent home on that first day of school. In the letter, I explain to the parents that it is all right for the students to call me at home. Sometimes the parents seem more shocked than the students. The parents and students really appreciate the extra support.

Unfortunately, there are teachers who believe their job ends when they walk out the school door at the end of the day. They worry about crank calls. They don't want to be bothered at home. And some feel it is the responsibility of the parents to deal with their child's homework.

It is kind of like a throwback to when doctors used to make house calls. Yes, there are times when it may be inconvenient, but as the "doctor," you can "cure" the problem and reduce everyone's stress levels. This availability has been particularly beneficial since we began a new math series that the parents had trouble understanding. As a professional educator, you should be willing to share your knowledge outside of the school setting.

A few weeks into the school year, it is good practice to contact any parents who you feel may need extra support or those for whom you may have questions regarding problems a student is having.

Prior to making a call, write down the specific issues you want to address. Be tactful but direct when you do talk to the parents. Instead of making "I" statements ("I think your child is having trouble sitting still in class."), use questions that encourage the parents to identify what they are seeing or feeling in regard to their child's problems ("Do you ever worry that Billy might be having trouble concentrating in school?").

Being proactive in making contact is another way to build good rapport with the parents. By initiating calls, you are sending a message to the parents that says you are concerned and want to do what is best for the child. This can be particularly effective with the "difficult" students in your class.

One of my favorite things to do when I have a student who is a borderline behavior problem and he or she has incurred some slight infraction is to call the parents while the child is standing next to me. Now normally, you would explain the situation to the parent, and the parent would probably get defensive with you or angry with the child—a negative contact for everyone involved. But what do you think would happen if, instead of a negative call, you tell the parent or parents some wonderful things about their child? For many parents of the "problem children," this is the first time they have ever heard anything positive about their child from the school! It may also be the first time a parent has had a positive experience with someone from a school.

After making the call, it is helpful to have a discussion with the child. You don't have to make any threats or try to cut any deals with the student. They are usually so confused it takes days for them to figure it out. Sometimes they are so guilt ridden, they break down and tell their parents what really happened.

The cornerstone to maintaining effective communication is a system of consistent documentation. It is not necessary to write down every contact, but it is essential to be disciplined enough to take the time to keep a phone and communication log. It is also not necessary to write long, detailed narratives for each contact. The teachers at Webster Stanley Elementary School use what we call the Red Binder. Each teacher keeps his or her own binder in the classroom.

We use a standard format for recording information. Primarily used for phone contacts, the form can also accommodate information from face-to-face meetings with either parents or students (or both), noting when written contacts were made and recording comments from any staff member who may also have pertinent information. There is one form for each student in the binder.

Codes are used to cut down on the amount of writing you need to do. Some examples are the following:

T = Teacher, S = Student, P = Parent, SS = School Staff; Check-off boxes for phone contact, face-to-face contact, or written contact; R = Issue resolved or O = Ongoing intervention; A = Academic issue, B = Behavior issue, O = Other (health concerns, interpersonal issues, etc.)

Dates, times, resources used, interventions attempted, and space for a brief narrative are included in the format. Because confidentiality is an issue with keeping this type of log, we are required to keep the Red Binder in a secure drawer or filing cabinet.

The documentation provides excellent information when it comes to developing and monitoring intervention plans, individual education plans, patterns in behavior, and academic concerns. The teacher can also use the information to analyze his or her own performance and then incorporate any modifications in such areas as teaching style and classroom management.

Even though you are still going to use written notes, do newsletters, and possibly communicate online, the telephone is your key tool in establishing and maintaining good home–school relations. By being willing to reach out to the students and parents, you will establish a bond based on working together to achieve positive results.

Helpful Tips

- Be proactive. Don't wait until a situation reaches the crisis point. If you have concerns, share them with the parents.
- Be willing to sacrifice some personal time by accepting calls at home from parents or students. Some of my most productive conversations with parents were done from my home.
- Take the time early in the year to find out the best times and preferred methods for contacting parents. Parents are more receptive to contacts if you are sensitive to their personal preferences.
- Get in the habit of maintaining a formalized communication log. Our memories are only so good, and little slips of paper tend to get lost.
- Get in the habit of making positive phone calls to the parents. Celebrating successes is something we need to do more often.
- Establish guidelines for calls made to your home by students or parents. Appropriate times when calls to your home can be made and acceptable topics should be identified in writing at the beginning of the school year.

CHAPTER 16

Relationships and Classroom Management

John McCleary

Ordway, Colorado

Teachers can employ many classroom management techniques on a daily basis. Although these are important, I also encourage the teachers I work with to consider one of the underlying issues that exists in every classroom in this country—the relationship between the teacher and the kids in his or her classroom.

Relationships mean everything to kids. If you don't believe me, all you have to do is follow a middle school student around for a day. What you'll see is that she largely defines herself and her position in school, her own self-worth, on how she relates to other students. People, personalities, and how they relate are king in a kid's life. Not to consider and evaluate your own relationship with students in your classroom and school is to overlook an essential component of classroom management.

Understandably, there are few tools or techniques that guide teachers through this important reflection. First, every classroom has its own unique chemistry, and likewise, each teacher is a unique individual with different expectations and needs. Because of this, you have to explore what kind of relationship you are going to have with students in your classroom. This might not be easy to do, especially when we leave traditional expectations and teacher-student roles to search for something more effective. Once you begin to figure out the relationship between you and your students, however, your classroom management will be much easier to accomplish.

Even better, when you build a strong relationship between yourself and your students, you create a foundation that supports learning, student achievement, and positive social development. You'll also improve your own working environment and create a career that is both rewarding and meaningful. I think there are four concepts that strong classroom managers incorporate into everything they do to help build a productive relationship that works well for both the student and the teacher.

Teachers who promote strong relationships between themselves and their students know that it is important to be yourself. There's probably a good reason you went into teaching, and hopefully it revolves around the idea that you feel like you have something meaningful to offer students. Even though it's important, I'm not talking about your subject area, but rather that something that makes you who you are. Make sure that you let these qualities shine during the school day. Do you have a great smile? Then smile! Do you have a good sense of humor? Then let it go!

Whatever, whoever you are, try to be that person and incorporate it into your classroom. This will accomplish two things. First, you'll feel more comfortable and more like the real, confident you. This will help with those tough decisions and defining parameters and how you deliver the subject material. Second, your students will sense that you are being genuine or real. In a world full of fakery, I've found that kids respect adults who aren't afraid to be their true selves.

A quality classroom relationship is also positive. A teacher who allows negativism to pervade his or her classroom undermines any successful relationship with students. A double standard exists when dealing with this topic. I have seen classrooms in which the teacher is mean, negative, and sarcastic and the students so quiet that you can hear the clock tick. The students appear to be on task—sitting in rows, doing whatever assignment is given to them—and the teacher is either at his or her desk or the front of the classroom grading papers or planning the next lesson. The image suggests that this classroom has strong management, but it is skewed. In reality, I would argue that it has no classroom management at all. When I first went into teaching, an old veteran grabbed my arm and gave me a piece of advice they never taught me in college. He looked at me seriously and said, "Listen, don't smile until Christmas." What he meant was that if I acted intimidating enough, I would solve a lot of my problems. No wonder so many kids hate school! In a negative environment, students are unwilling to take risks, unwilling to grow, and certainly unwilling to take anything meaningful away from the subject being forced on them. In today's performance-based, demanding educational environment, intimidating kids into being quiet and completing the day's worksheet is no longer enough. A negative teacher makes kids learn. A positive teacher in a positive environment leads kids toward learning.

A strong classroom relationship is also built on consistency. Students, especially those who may be more likely to cause classroom management challenges, react well to consistency and predictability. One of the most important things you can do as a teacher is to be in your classroom as often as possible. I've found that teachers who miss a lot of school days, whether because of professional development or "illness," have many more classroom management problems than do teachers who rarely miss a class. There are several reasons for this; first, students get the impression that you just don't care when you miss a lot of school. If you're not sure this is accurate, look at your own impressions of students who miss school on a regular basis.

Whether we accept it or not, I believe that students understand that the main prerogative of school is that they are there for learning above all other things. If the teacher is regularly absent, it's not difficult for students to construe that he or she might not care about teaching the subject and that maybe the learning isn't important. Also, when you're gone from the class, you've relegated the relationship you're trying to establish with students to a substitute teacher. Although they are important to the functioning of our school system, substitute teachers are rarely as effective or well trained as regular classroom teachers. Furthermore, outside of getting through the day, substitute teachers don't have the same commitment of establishing long-term meaningful relationships with the students in your classroom. Just as important, many of the discipline problems that cut into planning and personal time occur when a substitute is covering the class.

Teachers who build strong relationships in their classrooms also understand that problems are going to arise as the school year progresses. Teaching is a human business, and human beings run into problems. A successful classroom relationship between a teacher and his or her students is not defined by a lack of problems or even too many problems, but instead by how those problems are dealt with and resolved. It's also important to become effective at handling these classroom challenges. Students need to understand how you will react to anxieties about learning, disruption, motivational issues, and outright defiance. If you can develop a positive, consistent approach to problems, you'll find that they solve themselves just as quickly as they arise during the day.

Relationships are the foundation of a successful classroom management program. If you can find your own style in the classroom, be positive with the kids, show dedication through consistency, and deal with problems effectively in this same framework, teaching will always be a pleasant challenge.

CHAPTER 17

Turning Your Classroom Into a Purposeful Roller-Coaster Ride!

Dano Beal

Seattle, Washington

I simply love roller-coaster rides! There is something about the anticipation of the next drop, the thrill of the speed, the feeling of momentum through space. I want each day in my classroom to reach for these same attributes. As teachers, we are in continual competition with colorful, exotic outside forces that seem to provide instant gratification. Video games, television, computer simulations—all of these can entice children. So how can a classroom, or the teacher who inhabits it, compete with the highly stimulating world in which children are immersed today? An unidentified scholar once stated, "Those who think there is a difference between education and entertainment don't know the first thing about either one." I believe this quote to be among the greatest gifts I have ever received, and I count myself even more fortunate that it fell upon my ears during my first year of teaching. This simple quote has fueled and motivated my teaching style for more than fourteen years now. I discovered that I needed to provide the roller coaster, and, more important, the children needed to see me as the fuel that provides the momentum.

I remember the early Septembers of my career. I, like many teachers, faced the dilemma of "What do I put on the dastardly bulletin boards?" I had trouble identifying how random posters, district mantras, even random student work created a true "learning environment." Of course, there was a principal tapping her or his foot, expecting me to put up some sort of educational display before the first day of school. "Just cover the walls of your classroom"—that was the message.

Before entering teaching, I received a degree in theatre arts and set design. It always astounded me how one could create an environment on a stage using the craft of set design. Even more than that, how one could create a "feeling" that would permeate all who entered. Think of any live theatre piece that you may have seen. Perhaps you were immersed in the sultry, dark back alleys of Paris during *Les Miserables* or the bright, almost dizzying color of an *Oklahoma!* barn raising. I discovered that by creating a full-blown, detailed environment in my classroom, I am able to transport my students (and myself!) into any world that might be enticing me at the moment.

You will note that I chose to say a world that entices "me." Although some might feel that this is teacher centered, or perhaps even selfish, I offer this: Children look to us to help define what is exciting to them. I have found that when I create an environment that is challenging or mysterious to me, it automatically becomes magical to my students. Consider this example. Several years ago, I visited a museum while touring Greece. In a small corner of the museum was a collection of Egyptian artifacts, including an aged, decaying mummy. The exhibit included a wall that had been decorated with hieroglyphics and typical Egyptian designs. The curators had taken great care to recreate the feeling of an Egyptian archeological dig, even though the space was little more than the size of a typical American classroom. Upon returning to the States, I found myself wrestling with all sorts of questions about Egypt, mummification, and the mysteries of an archeological adventure. I began to envision ways that I could use my classroom to learn more about an Egyptian tomb. I set out to recreate the interior of such a place—*on the wall of Room 26!* I began about three weeks before the start of school, redesigning the interior of my classroom. I put up aged, weathered beams made of donated wood and industrial cardboard, painted the walls with rectangular stones, airbrushed for a smoky authenticity. I blackened windows, installed electric candles, and lowered the ceiling with cargo netting.

The reading corner was redesigned with angled walls, covered with sandpaper and authentic hieroglyphics. On an upper bookshelf, I had a small dish for burning incense because, as I had learned, Egyptian tombs had a smell. I used parchment paper to write up our daily schedules, lunchroom menus, and rules. Piles of dusty, stained gauze were lurking in hidden corners to suggest possible tomb robbing. Papier-mâché urns lined the walls, and storage boxes were stacked, strapped in old leather and hemp rope. I placed battery-operated torches at the doorway to the classroom. Our entry way was also painted and constructed in the style of the pyramid, allowing the "set" of our classroom to spill out into the hallway, thus enticing all who passed by to enter and share in the adventure of the unknown.

On the first day of school, the students were greeted by the stranger who would be their teacher for the next nine months—an "Indiana Jones" character, dressed and already immersed in the adventure! Every child entered, wide-eyed and curious, wondering what was going to happen next. The parents lingered, amazed at what they were looking at, whispering, "This sure isn't what school was like when I was in second grade!" Our yearlong exploration was off and running! Within the first two hours of school, the class had stuffed a small salmon with melon seeds, lovingly wrapped it in salt and gauze. This was our class "mummy," which hung from the ceiling for nine months waiting to be unwrapped on the final day of school . . . everyone wants to know what an unwrapped mummy looks like, right?

As you can see, the entire room was redesigned, using myriad donated and purchased supplies. The trick to success is in the attention to detail. The more detailed the set, the more authentic the environment. On hot August days, it's not uncommon to see little eyes peering through the windows hoping for a glimpse of what the new design will be. On the first day of school, the classroom is filled to the brim with past students, families, and even district staff, curious as to what Mr. Beal has had up his sleeve. The classroom set is always kept secret until the first bell rings on opening day. Anticipation is a powerful fuel!

Often, observers in my classroom will ask how I bring the environmental set into the daily curriculum. Exactly how does a teacher use an Egyptian tomb to teach everyday addition and subtraction? Or how do you tie together the scientific properties of liquids and life along the Nile? I have found that educators are masters at making connections—or they should be! By consistently modeling the search for connections in the world around us, our students will begin to do the same. I truly believe that this search is at the center of lifelong learning. A masterful teacher will bring the environmental "set" into all aspects of the classroom, using computer graphics on assignments, introducing lessons with dramatic flair such as a monologue in the style of an ancient pharaoh or slave, or writing assignments that include the occasional hieroglyphic. Madeline Hunter touted the importance of the Anticipatory set. I say, take that Anticipatory set and run with it—*decorate* it, *embellish* it, *magnify* it, and *celebrate* it to its absolute saturation point!

Benefits of the Environmental "Set" Approach to Classroom Design

- Increased student (and teacher!) engagement
- Increased parent support
- Continual community and business involvement
- A foundation for all curricula to "spoke" from
- Lower incidence of disruptive behavior
- Provides a foundation for yearlong exploration
- Less bulletin board maintenance!
- Increased opportunities for cooperative exploration and activities

Helpful Tips

Because the creation of such a classroom is so labor and material intensive, I plan on the environment staying in place for the entire school year. It is vital that the initial idea be broad and that it provide motivation for the long haul. The teacher must search out ways to saturate the classroom with the chosen theme. Solicit friends, family, businesses, and librarians for morsels that become the finishing details. For the teacher, the rewards will last throughout the year; for the student, a lifetime.

Please understand, this approach can be expensive, in terms of both time and money. During the early summer months, I find myself planning and imagining what the next year's "set" is going to look like. I take a part-time summer job to finance my designs, because it is not unusual for my receipts to surpass $2,000. It is important to keep in mind that I consider this a high-yield investment. I also depend heavily on the generosity of the business community. I never hesitate to ask for donations of supplies or curricula. I search garage sales, attics, thrift stores, and wholesale closeouts. The trick is to always be on the lookout for materials, and to think creatively. It boils down to what the Walt Disney Company calls "Imagineering." The combination of imagination and engineering, or more specifically, doing what it takes to bring your imagination closer to reality.

Need some ideas? Let your imagination soar! Over the years I have imagined, created, and rotated several environments, including the following:

A Space Station

The Secret Garden

A Wild West Ghost Town

A Tall-Sail Ship

Hollywood of the '20s and '30s

A Hopi Indian Pueblo

An Egyptian Pyramid

Under the Australian Great Barrier Reef

A Fairy Tale Forest

King Arthur's Great Hall

A Candy Factory

Michelangelo's Studio

In closing, I sincerely hope that all teachers will continue to ride roller coasters and never forget that education and entertainment should always journey together, hand in hand!

CHAPTER 18

Classroom Discipline

Keith Ballard

San Diego, California

A s an educator who is the recipient of more than thirty teaching awards, the Milken Educational award being the most recent, many educators have asked me for advice on teaching in the classroom. Currently, I teach five classes of mariachi music—"the music of Mexico"—and one class of steel drum band at Montgomery Middle School (MMS). I interface with approximately 160 students on a given day. The school is located approximately two miles from the San Diego, California–Tijuana, Mexico, international border. The student population is very diverse with more than 80 percent of the students being of Hispanic descent.

I have found that exemplary teaching and learning can take place only if a foundation of exemplary discipline strategies has been established within the classroom. Although I teach music, the discipline strategies that I utilize in my classroom could be applied to almost any classroom in the nation.

I received my B.S. in music education in 1993 from Arizona State University. Like most university programs that prepare future educators, I was required to take many classes in the theory of teaching. I was not able to apply the educational theory that I learned until my student teaching practicum. Much of the educational theory that I learned in college did not seem to work in the classroom, particularly the strategies that I learned in classroom management.

The high school teacher that I was assigned to work with to do my student teaching was average at best, and his classroom discipline was poor. This student teaching assignment provided me with a valuable learning experience regarding the things that should not be done in the classroom. The mediocrity that permeated this high school music program reinforced in me why a strong discipline program needed to be in place.

Following my high school student teaching assignment, I was assigned to Hendrix Junior High School in Mesa, Arizona. The cooperating teacher that I would work with for a semester was Doug Akie. It became apparent to me during my first week working with Doug that he was an expert musician as well as a master teacher. His junior high school bands played like the best high school bands in the state, and his top band had received national honors. Although Doug had an incredible work ethic, it was his discipline strategies that he incorporated in the classroom that placed his students in a class above the rest. It was at Hendrix Junior High School that I developed the discipline strategies that would allow me to be a successful educator working with a diverse lower-economic student population.

Over the course of the past six years, I have worked with approximately twenty educators. All but one seemed to be competent in their knowledge of the subject, and these teachers appeared to be dedicated educational professionals. The majority of their problems in the classroom centered on discipline. A question that I always asked each one of these educators was, Should a classroom be modeled after a democracy? The response from approximately 40 percent of these educators—and virtually every student—to whom I have posed this question was that a classroom should, in fact, be modeled after a democracy.

Discipline Strategy 1: Classrooms Aren't Democracies

To create a workable and stable democracy, individuals must have the emotional and intellectual maturity to understand the responsibilities that democracy entails. They also need the knowledge and skills that will permit them to make rational, moral choices that are in the best interest of society as a whole and not just in their own interests. The fact of the matter is that educating the young cannot be done in a democratic environment because true participation and shared decision making will prevent teachers from fulfilling their proper role. Most students also lack the maturity, knowledge, and skills that would be needed to create a democracy. Schools must be places where students can participate, but they cannot be places where everyone participates equally.

It is important to let the students know from day one that your class does not operate in the same manner that a democracy does.

Discipline Strategy 2: The Teacher Is the Authority

Teachers who exercise their authority use all of the tools at their disposal to help their students learn. Teachers who exercise their authority take responsibility for their class and are always prepared. In many cases, well-prepared lesson plans that actively engage the students will cut down on many discipline problems. Most students really do want to learn and enjoy a class that emphasizes structure, regimentation, and discipline.

It is not only teachers' right to exercise their authority in the classroom; more important, it is their responsibility. In efforts to make public schooling more "democratic" and student centered, we have seriously undermined the authority of the teacher and thus lowered the educational expectations in the eyes of both the students and the public at large. By trying to foster student self-esteem, many teachers have in fact undermined students' self-esteem—and their own.

To remind the students in my classroom that I am the authority in charge of the classroom at all times, I have a large poster that hangs at the front of my classroom. This sign states, "Students, being a part of the mariachi class is not like going to Burger King. Here, you will not have it your way. You will have it my way, or you will not have it at all!!!"

Discipline Strategy 3: Students Prefer a Teacher Who Is "Demanding" Over "Caring"

Maintaining high standards and discipline in the classroom will actually foster student self-esteem. Most students actually respect a teacher who is more demanding than caring. I have told my students many times, "It is my job to be demanding and for you to learn. You will respect me for my efforts. There is nothing in my teaching contract that says that we have to be friends or, for that matter, that we have to get along with one another. If we do become friends, it will be a bonus for both of us."

▧ Discipline Strategy 4: Require All of Your Students and Their Parents to Sign a Discipline Contract

Having high disciplinary, as well as academic, expectations for students is one of the most caring things that you can do for them. Make sure that the parents and students understand your expectations, rules, and the consequences. Clearly post your rules on the wall of your classroom. *I personally interface with every one of my parents and require them and their child to sign a contract stating that they have read and understand my classroom rules, expectations, and consequences.* Because many of the parents at my school speak only Spanish, the contracts are printed in both Spanish and English. Most of the parents may not read this material, but their signature on the contract will be beneficial if you have a problem with them or their child during the school year.

▧ Discipline Strategy 5: Enforce Your Classroom Rules, Expectations, and Consequences

From day one, you must enforce your classroom rules. *It is imperative that if you say you are going to do something, you do it!* Many teachers fail in the area of enforcement because they consistently fail to follow through with consequences. Consistency is the name of the game. The rules are only as good as the person who will enforce them.

▧ Discipline Strategy 6: Gain Credibility as a Teacher With the Principal and Assistant Principal

Make sure that your school site administration understands you are a concerned and dedicated teacher. Give them a copy of your classroom contract and ask that they read it. It is important to let them know that you plan to take care of your classroom discipline problems. Most likely, they will be happy to hear this. *In the event that you may need their assistance, it is important to gain a commitment from them that they will support you in a situation that requires the enforcement of your classroom discipline policies.*

CHAPTER 19

Acquiring and Utilizing Technology Devices in the Elementary Classroom

Teresa Morton Owens

Blountsville, Alabama

E very state and district curriculum guide dictates that effective utilization of technology is essential to every classroom. Written on paper, this appears an enthralling commitment to learning. It allows the reader to visualize a tranquil and worry-free setting where all children have access to computers or whatever else the teacher has access to in his or her classroom. In most schools, teachers still have the creative license to explore and teach according to that inner, God-given ability to inspire the learner. If this is the case in your school, then take advantage of the learning environment that you can still control.

With the gamut of technology devices spiraling from the obsolete overhead projector to the current classroom use of personal digital assistants (PDAs), teachers are at a turning point for classroom instruction with the presentation tools they model and use in curriculum delivery methods. Students in our society are not interested in the bland instructional delivery that most of us grew up witnessing. If we are to change the world, we must change our modes of teaching.

Lecture is out. Discovery is in. Sound too revolutionary? It shouldn't. Teachers have been inundated with discovery science for years. It is proven that children who have the ability to explore and discover actually learn. As an educator, however, it is much easier to stand in one location and tell information to the kids. But what in your teaching career has ever been easy?

I use the following theory with my own learning: I believe that, given enough time, anyone can master any device. This is the approach I have taken with technology. I remember a college class in which it was actually predicted that within the next ten years (keep in mind, this was 1979), people would possess computers in their homes. Undaunted by such "prophecies," I kept typing on my typewriter, with correction fluid close at hand. When I started teaching twenty-three years ago, I was hired as a K–12 gifted education specialist. I was given one of only two computers that existed in my county school district to use with my classes. This was big—not just the ideal, but the computer itself. It was an old TRS-80 with a tape drive. It took thirty minutes to warm it up and the same amount of time to change programs. Teaching in a pullout program, one is limited to shortened class periods during the course of a day. Thus to alternate from high school to first-grade programs, it took one complete class period for the computer to recognize the change. I've said all of this to give readers some insight into my patience with computers and technology.

Teachers have to experience a comfort zone in the computer tech world. As a teacher, you can't be afraid of tearing it up. You have to go in and explore the technology to teach children about it.

Take into consideration kids' learning styles today. Not all children are so well equipped at home that they have all the trendy computer devices, but most of them have access to Nintendo and PlayStation. Even in my school, where the socioeconomic status is low-middle income, a majority of the students own these tech toys. Therefore, students are somewhat predisposed with a "technology capability" that enables them to stand toe-to-toe when confronted with technological updates. Why shouldn't they be tech savvy? They have been surrounded by the world of technology since day one.

Thus why would a teacher want to teach without the most comprehensive and up-to-date technology possible? My belief in this has made me a sort of "technology guru" at my school. My kids know that I do this for them. I believe getting them to listen and pay attention is highly correlated with my presenting lessons with energy and enthusiasm and in an interesting manner. For a nine-year-old, interest is fleeting. Even for me, if I'm bored with it, chances are my students are also. In my classroom, I have every tech device possible. If there is even a remote chance of using something new, I will work to submit a grant that enables me to acquire it from whatever source is convenient.

Trade shows are excellent venues of exploration in the tech-teaching world. Great state-of-the-art gadgets are waiting to be discovered by teachers. Trained salespeople are always on hand to perform live demonstrations. I purchased my FlexCam video camera (VideoLabs) from a vender at a trade show. In addition, sometimes there is a discount for purchases made from a show. This is more beneficial than ordering online or from a catalog. Technology institutes are another source for tech equipment introductions. One of the best discoveries I have made was at a local in-district technology institute. This is where I found out about SMARTBoards (more about SMARTBoards later). At the same in-district technology workshop, I was introduced to the CPS (Classroom Performance System). Recently, I won another grant that enabled me the opportunity to purchase some PDAs. Overall, I have acquired lots of tech "devices" that my kids deem innovative enough to hold their attention.

The FlexCam was my first acquisition after purchasing a computer and television with my class's fundraising money. This purchase enabled my students to view a projected image on the screen. They also could videotape reports and show them to the class. This "eye in the sky" proved effective when I had to slip out for a restroom break, as well. On particularly rowdy days, I'd point the FlexCam toward my class and tell them the camera was focused on them. With the television off, students were puzzled as to whether I was taping their behavior or not. Further, the FlexCam would function as an opaque projector, without the chore of making a transparency. But this was before the SMARTBoard.

I have one overwhelming belief: SMARTBoards are God's gift to teachers for all of their unpaid overtime work. After I was introduced to SMARTBoards, I was determined that I would have one in my classroom. If you haven't seen one in action, find a trade show and locate the SMART Technologies booth. SMARTBoards are touch-sensitive projection screens that can be written on with a large stylus. The color background possibilities are endless. Sometimes, when my class seems to be asleep, neon green is the color of the day. In addition, surfing the Net on a seventy-two-inch screen is fantastic. Students can read the Internet pages from the back of the room without squinting. Studying history and need a map? Just pull up the templates. Voila! You have a political map or just an outline that students can fill in or color or match to the country. Kids can tap the word and drag it across the map to the correct location. Furthermore, SMARTBoards are equipped with handwriting recognition and can take a student's handwriting and transform it into any typed font; perfect for e-mailing an E-Pal who lives in Canada.

I guess you are wondering how I financed this, what with spending most of my grocery money on the other essential things my school kids constantly need? The answer was found at the Web site www.smarterkids .org. From that first district tech show, I learned about a foundation that would partially fund the price of SMARTBoards for use in the classroom. At an approximately 10 percent discount, I decided I would fill out the online application. A few days later, I discovered another program from the same foundation that teamed a fifth- and a sixth-grade teacher together for a program called Connections. This program not only funded a SMARTBoard and multimedia projector for the participating classes but also funded training opportunities for each teacher in Calgary, Alberta, Canada. I opted to apply for Connections, with little thought that my grant application would be selected. Thus on April 1, 2001, my teaching partner, Tina, and I were informed that we had been selected. I would be flying to Canada in July of that summer for training, and Tina would visit the following year. If that wasn't enough, during the duration of the program, several of our students would be flown, along with us on a second visit, to meet other students from classrooms across the United States and Canada who also participated in Connections activities. At press time, eight electrified students are busy planning their first flights as a unique learning experience thanks to the Connections program and SMART Technologies.

Another funding source I used was acquiring National Certification. In some states, monetary incentives are in place for successful completion of this process. In November 2001, I received notification that I had achieved this special recognition. At this time, it meant a one-time $5,000 classroom grant. (Check to see what incentives are offered in your state.) This is the source I used to purchase my CPS devices. If you have watched *America's Funniest Videos* where the audience votes on remote keypads, you have seen the CPS program. With this learning system, I can input any questionnaire, assessment, trivia questions, and so forth, into my computer, display it on a surface, and my students can input their answers with the remote keypads. The use of this technology does so much for a "ho-hum" vocabulary checkup or even a math quiz. In fact, my students actually remind me that we need to "do our test."

Anything to invigorate and enrich the learning environment is well worth the time and effort of writing a grant proposal. The Unsung Heroes Award is a competitive grant program sponsored by the ING Corporation. During the fall of 2002, I learned that my grant application for handheld computers would be funded through the Unsung Heroes Grant. Now my students are exposed to the use of PDAs in their writing instruction. It was a pleasant surprise to watch my students finish an expository paper on the PDA faster than their counterparts did on conventional computers.

In conclusion, if you dream it, you can attain it. Nothing is out of reach for those who want to instill a love of the learning process in their students. To achieve this dream, teachers have to go the extra mile and *make* dreams come true. Furthermore, without support from within the school system, teachers would be stymied by lukewarm and obsolete instructional techniques and equipment. I have been fortunate to have the support of my principal and district superintendents in the application processes that are involved with grant proposals. With education funding in financial arrears nationwide, determined teachers can still acquire a caviar classroom, even in a Chapter I school where 80 percent of the students qualify for the federal free and reduced lunch program.

CHAPTER 20

Round-Robin Learning Groups

A Classroom Management Alternative

Gail McGoogan

St. Cloud, Florida

"**C**an we play again tomorrow?" shouted one of my third graders as we reflected on the day's activities. Oh my goodness, I thought. If these thirty-two students go home and tell their parents that we played all day and are going to have a repeat the next day, I am in deep trouble—trouble with a capital T! However, he was right: The day had flown and didn't seem like work at all.

First, the perception of what happened that day needs to be clarified. "Tell me what you did today as you played," I responded. He proceeded to name what he did in math, science, and so on. Soon others were adding their new-found knowledge. Finally, from the back of the group one surprised voice cried out, "We did everything we know!" We all realized that learning can take place even when having *fun*. The key, of course, is classroom management.

We know that classroom management comes in a multitude of configurations. Some we embrace, others cause us to shake our heads and ask, "How does anybody learn anything in that classroom?" My experience is that any number of configurations is appropriate depending on one's goals. In my classroom, on any given day, one might encounter an individual working quietly, collaborative groups conversing, a student lecturing, or teams of two or three investigating a scientific principle.

My students and I do have a favorite method, however: *Round-Robin Learning Groups.* As they work in these groups, all disciplines occur simultaneously all day. What may look disorganized to an outsider makes complete sense to my students who learn to be self-starters, independent learners, and teachers. It causes them to enter the room, look at the planning board, and say, "Oh good! We're doing small groups today!"

▧ Managing "Who" and "What"

The first question that comes to mind is, "How do students cover all content using small groups?" They begin with one subject and rotate through the others as the day progresses. Actually, *the class becomes four or five separate classes with each group beginning the day with a different subject.*

Example

Math
(Red, Blue, Yellow, Green)

Science
(Blue, Yellow, Green, Red)

Social Studies
(Yellow, Green, Red, Blue)

Language Arts
(Green, Red, Blue, Yellow)

In my class, each child's desk has a colored smiley face that identifies a group and order of rotation. From time to time, I change their colored stickers, so they have an opportunity to work closely with a number of students. Do they always like their study buddies? Of course not. The real world expects them to collaborate and get a job done whether or not they "love" their fellow worker. My response to complaints is, "You have a job to do. It is your choice. How do *you* want to handle it?" It is amazing how attitudes change when students must take responsibility for their own actions. It has been my experience that after one or two complaints, I don't hear any more, and students develop a sense of camaraderie.

As you can see, each group starts with a different discipline and rotates as the day progresses. When I repeat the small-group learning either the next day or some other time, I rotate the "rotations" by taking the top Red, Blue, or other color, moving it to the bottom, and inching each other configuration up one discipline. Each group has an opportunity to start with a different subject each day.

Tip

Once group participants are chosen, don't change them in midstream. Keep them as they are for the day. This gives students an opportunity to work out problems and share successes.

▧ Managing "When"

The second question I am usually asked is how I schedule the day. I play with the numbers. Take the total time for the day, subtract teaching time, divide by the number of groups or amount of time for each group—and there you have it.

Example

8:40–8:50	Attendance/Morning Announcements/Lunch Count
8:50–9:20	**Minilessons (Instructions for Day)**
9:20–10:00	**Rotation 1**
10:05–10:45	**Rotation 2**
10:50–11:30	**Rotation 3**

11:34–12:25	Lunch/Recess
12:30–1:00	DEAR Time (Silent Reading)
1:00–1:40	**Rotation 4**
1:45–2:30	Block Time (PE, Music, Art, etc.)
2:30–2:45	Homework Assignments/Prepare for Dismissal
2:45–3:20	Read To/**Reflection**
3:20	Dismissal

True, one of the drawbacks is that the day is broken into small increments with little to no flexibility. Using skills across the curriculum minimizes this shortcoming, however, and ensures a rich experience for all students.

My lesson plan book looks the same for small groups as any other teaching modality; one cannot tell what the configuration for the day will be. The deciding factor is what I want to accomplish.

Tip

Make certain you have planned enough content for each rotation. Not enough is a much greater problem than too much, because inactivity can cause discipline problems no matter how much students enjoy small-group rotations. You can always complete what was not finished the next day.

▨ Managing the "Big Picture"

Students must know where to go when and what to bring when they go there. Because remembering is too great a task to ask of students and teacher, one dry-erase board is set up for Round-Robin Learning Groups where I list what we do, when we do it, and materials and texts needed.

Example

Column One   Content and Happy Faces as listed in "Managing 'Who' and 'What'"

Column Two   Assignments for the day

Science: Activity "Force and Motion," pp. F34 & F35. Perform activity and record in science log. Continue listing all content to be covered for the day.

Column Three   *Materials:* Science text, science log, pencil

Column Four   Time schedule

1   9:20–10:00
2   10:05–10:45
3   10:50–11:30
4   1:00–1:40

All new content is taught and assignments explained during the "Minilesson" at the beginning of the day. The five minutes between rotations is for cleanup—we always leave an area the way we found it—and reflection. We discuss what we learned and "words of wisdom" we have for the class. Specific answers to problems are not allowed; however, management information and opinions are welcomed. I then review what is expected, and the students go on to the next content area.

Tip

Schedule content so there is a balance of independent study, quiet areas, and teacher conferencing. You cannot monitor all areas, all day. Have confidence in your students and their ability to collaborate constructively. This will free you, for example, to complete in one day those writing conferences that used to take all week. Or to give attention to Johnny's math or reading. Or . . .

▨ Managing the Classroom Setup

The study areas are defined by what is to be accomplished in each area. For instance, some take a math test while others participate in student-teacher writing conferences. Another group conducts a science experiment as the final group investigates research for social studies.

Careful consideration must be given to quiet areas, so testing and writing groups are placed close to each other. Collaborative areas for sharing and experimenting and computer areas for research are scattered to keep the noise at a minimum. The physical configuration depends on the goals for the day.

Tip

Arrive early on the days of small-group rotations to guarantee the room is ready when students arrive. Setting up takes time; however, the day has a way of running itself with little confusion and minimum intervention from you when you and the room are prepared.

Managing Behavior

This is the easiest part of small-group rotations. In my experience, students love being part of something different. They also enjoy collaboration and the independence this type of learning affords them. Nothing is more disturbing than to be an observer rather than a participant. So if one misbehaves, I simply tap the student on the shoulder and say, "You just lost your privilege." The next step is to return to an unoccupied desk to complete the work individually. If an activity, such as for a science experiment, should happen to require materials, "Oh well. I'm sorry. You should have thought of that when you made your choice." After one student has this experience, not many follow.

Example

On the first day of school, we start out with a simple experiment to begin scientific thinking and data recording in our science logs. One year, as we sat on the balcony outside our second-floor classroom, a new student, angry because the draw of the lot put him in a group of girls and damaged his "macho" image, was not cooperating. When asked why, he said, "I ain't got nothin' to write with."

"Oh," I commented. "And where is your pencil?"

"Down there," he indicated, pointing to the edge of the balcony.

"How did it get 'down there'?" I asked. To which he answered, "It fell."

"You are too far from the edge of the balcony for it to fall. What really happened?" Then I stood and waited for an answer. Finally, he flicked his fingers indicating that the "fall" had been given considerable help.

"Can I go down and get it?" Now he had a way to desert his group and wander around for a while.

"No," I responded and asked two girls to get his pencil. Then I said, "You have just lost your privilege. Please go to your desk." He understood exactly what had happened and returned to the classroom. When he had no data to record and share, besides not getting to blow bubbles because we were testing blower shapes versus bubble shapes, he was not a happy camper. He did learn a lesson, however. If I had said, "If you do that one more time . . . ," knowing Andy, the year would have been one "one more time" after another. We went on from that time of testing to a very productive relationship.

Tip

Make behavior rules few and simple, then follow through with consequences. "If you do that one more time . . ." guarantees "one more time." When lessons have real meaning for the students, they don't want to miss the experience and behavior becomes a minor issue, especially with special needs students.

Round-Robin Learning Groups: The Ups and Downs

On the Down Side

- Scheduling restraints leave no time for flexibility. One cannot "run over," or the next group is shortchanged.
- Completing class and materials setup before students arrive makes the beginning of the teacher's day busy.
- Placing all materials where students have easy access and can return them at the end of the rotation takes planning and practice.
- Clarifying goals for the day so that not just fun takes place, but also meaningful learning, is a great responsibility.

On the Up Side

- Using skills across the curriculum removes the shortcoming of time restraints.
- Setting up the day before students arrive frees you to circulate, teach, or facilitate. Some days the students are so absorbed in their activities and assisting one another, they don't seem to need you.
- Relinquishing responsibility for learning develops independent critical thinkers and allows your students to take pride in their accomplishments.
- Acquiring materials is more manageable because you need enough for five or six instead of twenty-five (e.g., microscopes, math manipulatives, research materials, computers).

There are many ways to be successful in the classroom. I find that when using a variety of learning configurations, all my students succeed. The days *they* like best and on which they accomplish the most, however, are the days when we play: the days we participate in Round-Robin Learning Groups.

CHAPTER 21

Computer Lab Policies and Procedures

Cynthia R. Murray

Covington, Louisiana

I am a twenty-five-year veteran teacher and am presently employed as a business teacher/school-to-work coordinator at Covington High School in Covington, Louisiana. Currently, I teach keyboarding, keyboarding applications, business computer applications, and mentor a school-based enterprise (Print Shop) in which my class interns are responsible for all our in-school printing. I am also a technology trainer for St. Tammany Parish. Through the years, I have experimented with many computer lab policies and procedures and hope that the following tips and insights will be helpful to other colleagues.

With a thirty-seat-capacity computer lab, I have found that if I institute policies and procedures at the beginning of each semester, the year will run much more smoothly. When I first started teaching in a lab situation, there were no written procedures to follow, and the classroom setting was literally chaos. The policies and procedures that I discuss here have evolved over many years.

Research shows that students want and appreciate structure, and sometimes the classroom is the only place a student will be introduced to it. Less learning takes place in classrooms that are not structured to some degree than in classrooms with policies and procedures because students disrupt their peers' learning. A teacher should be the one in control of learning in the classroom.

At the beginning of each semester, my computer policies and procedures are reviewed and practiced each day for at least a week. At the end of the week, I test the students on their understanding of these rules. Some of the most effective computer lab procedures I have implemented consist of the following practices.

At the beginning of each semester, I assign a computer seating chart. No student is allowed to move or change computers unless he or she has my permission. By instituting a seating chart, I can take roll after the students begin their assignments, I can learn the students' names more easily, and, if a computer breaks down or vandalism occurs, I know who was the last person to sit at that particular computer workstation.

Each week I appoint two student monitors to distribute and pick up student folders and data disks. As my students enter the computer lab, I expect them to sign in at their designated workstations, be seated, check their workstations to be sure all equipment is in proper working order, and begin working by the time the tardy bell rings. After the students begin working, I record attendance, take care of computer malfunctions, and assist students who have been absent. If I need to obtain my students' attention for discussion, I blink the lights once. This procedure alerts the students to become quiet and listen to directions for the day.

Each Monday, I distribute a weekly assignment sheet that shows what my students should be working on and the time frame in which to complete the assignments. If I need to have a technique demonstration using projection equipment, I indicate this on their assignment sheet using asterisks, and the students move to their assigned seats in the middle of the room for the demo and questions. If a teacher does not have desks in the center of the room, he or she may have the students turn off their monitors and turn their chairs around for the demonstration. This procedure ensures that students will not be working on their computers while the teacher gives directions and explains techniques.

Another procedure I follow is to place flags on the front of the students' monitors. These flags consist of three small sheets of different-colored laminated construction paper held together by a brad that allows the flags to move. When the students have a question, they raise a certain-colored flag depending on the urgency of the question. For example, a red flag means an extremely urgent question that cannot wait, a yellow flag means the student has a question but can continue to work until I am able to get to them, and a blue flag means that a student is printing or having technical difficulty with his or her computer.

Many of the teachers that I have taught agonize about what to do when a student finishes his or her assignments early. I have implemented two options for my classes: First, they can circulate around the room and help me answer other students' questions. This enables the student monitor to have a more in-depth understanding of the concepts just learned because they are explaining them to their peers. Second, the students can work on their MOUS (Microsoft Office User Specialist) Diploma Endorsement Certification. By completing the coursework, the students can complete an online exam through the Microsoft Corporation, and, if they pass, obtain their MOUS certification.

I have found that by following these policies and procedures, more learning takes place; the confusion, distractions, and noise levels have been significantly lowered; behavior problems have diminished; and the students stay on task longer and ultimately become more self-disciplined, responsible learners.

Computer Lab Sign-In Sheet (ROOM 403)

Week of February 9–13, 2004

	1st Hour	2nd Hour	3rd Hour	4th Hour	5th Hour	6th Hour	7th Hour
Monday							
Tuesday							
Wednesday							
Thursday							
Friday							

Helpful Tips

Tips for Secondary Classroom Management

- Get the class started before you begin record keeping.
- Distribute a weekly assignment sheet or post assignments.
- Provide a student folder (with individual names) for every student to keep all handouts, printed work, and graded papers in the classroom.
- Every student should be seated in his or her assigned seat and working when the tardy bell rings.
- When students are absent, place assignment sheet, handouts, or cover sheets in their student folders so that they do not have to ask what they missed. Indicate on the makeup work if student needs to see the teacher.
- All students should stay seated until class is dismissed to avoid confusion and horseplay.
- A limited number of bathroom passes may be given out. Have students put their names on the back to reduce the temptation of theft. If not used, these passes could be turned in at the end of the semester for extra credit.
- Post homework on e-boards or your school's Web site.
- All book bags, purses, and so on, should be stored under the student's computer station or desk to facilitate teacher movement around the room.
- Allow students who finish their assignments early to act as monitors and help slower students.

Tips for Computer Lab Management

- On the first day of school, assign a seating chart for each computer workstation.
- Discuss your Classroom Rules and Procedures—post these!
- Post your seating chart the first week of school.
- On each computer, place a three-part (each part a different colored piece of paper) flag for students' questions to minimize talking distractions.

- Designate certain days during the week to print assignments, which minimizes confusion and movement in the classroom.
- Have students turn in specified assignments with a Cover Sheet attached to the front. The Cover Sheet indicates what is to be turned in, the order in which the assignments should be stapled, and certain points to be sure and check before the student prints.
- Always have a teacher-directed Internet search. Include a handout indicating the Web site address, questions to answer, and a Web site evaluation.

CHAPTER 22

Overinvolved Parents

Pauline H. Jacroux

Kailua, Hawaii

E very morning in my first-grade classroom, I check the clothespins
left pinned to the edge of the Homework Box to see which children
have not yet turned in their homework.

"Freddie, where is your homework?"

An all too frequent reply is, "My mother forgot to put it in my
backpack."

My all-time favorite answer, however, is, "Oh, my mother didn't
finish doing it yet."

I teach in a school where many of the parents are overinvolved in
their children's lives, denying them opportunities to make their own decisions, learn from their mistakes, be responsible for their own belongings,
and ultimately be responsible for their own learning. The child's name
and sometimes the work is written in the parent's handwriting. One
mother drove her son to school, parked the car, walked him to the classroom, helped him settle in and do his morning job, and came to me saying, "*We* aren't sure how to do this job," went home, packed a home
lunch, returned to school and brought the lunch all the way to the classroom, and placed it in the Lunch Basket quietly while I taught.

A father rushed home before school to fetch his daughter's PE shoes so that she wouldn't have to run the extra jog that comes as a consequence of being without proper shoes. He then went back a second time to make and bring a home lunch.

I have started school in the morning with several parents still in the classroom making friends with the students or chatting with one another. At the end of the day, I sometimes have parents mingling outside or even looking in my doors before the dismissal bell rings. Parents ask me where to put their child's things. They come to help during class parties and end up sitting in their child's chair with the child on their lap. Last week I saw a former student who is now in the fourth grade being carried by her mother while shopping.

These overinvolved parents are to be admired for the care, concern, and time given for their children. Does that mean that the other parents don't care as much? Certainly not! The other parents have a belief in their children's ability to learn to take care of themselves and be responsible citizens at a young age. They are able to see down the road a bit and anticipate the pride they will feel in the accomplishments of their offspring. They can see their child growing into a unique individual, not a reflection or extension of themselves. They nurture and encourage rather than "do for" or "wait on" their children.

What is the result of such overinvolvement? First of all, the parents tend to ask frequently (remember, they are waiting outside the door) about how their child is doing. All they want to hear is the good stuff. If the teacher suggests areas for improvement, their tendency is to think that the teacher is picking on their child or that this is a negatively run classroom. They also tend to expect turnaround behavior in a day or two because they have discussed the problem with their child and he or she understands. So they ask every day or two for an update, expecting that good news each time.

Among the behaviors that I see in the classroom are children who are not careful listeners. They have always relied on Mom or Dad to get the directions. They are not organized and don't know where their belongings are or what is in their backpack. They forget to check in, turn in their homework, return their library books, wear PE shoes on the proper days, or bring in permission forms, money, or bag lunches on field trip days. They expect an immediate replacement for things they have lost or broken. (That includes pencils they have cut in two with their scissors or on which they have bitten off the erasers, portfolios they have torn, and art materials they have misused by not following directions.)

They often ask for and expect rewards for favors they perform. When I explain the homework, they ask, with a note of panic in their voices, "Does my mom know what to do?" They tend to report the negative occurrences in school to their parents because that gets parental attention, maybe even a parental note or visit to the school to defend them. They tend not to be academic risk takers; that is, if they have a spelling question, they won't continue writing until someone spells the word for them, or they won't try to solve a problem without help at their side.

Helpful Tips

Each year one of the school newsletters addresses the issue of parents hanging around the classrooms during school hours. A request is made that they drop their child at the front of the school in the morning. There, the principal and some educational aides are posted to open car doors and escort children to the sidewalk, or even become the Mary Poppins Brigade by hustling them to shelter with umbrellas! In the afternoon, this same procedure occurs in reverse.

In response, the school has received letters from irate parents saying that the walk to the classroom is their bonding time with their child. Or, I know I should allow this, but he's my baby! Or, Why is it that at preschool the parents are so welcome and when the children get to kindergarten we are told to leave? They want to know everything that is happening with their child and can't stand being away. One mother cruised the street alongside our playground at recess time to watch her daughter.

As a first-grade teacher, I always allow for a period of adjustment. Then I mention in my own class newsletter to parents, "The Dragon Breath" (because we read about a baby dragon at the start of school, not because of the image of myself I am trying to project to the parents), how the children need their own time in the morning to connect with their classmates, to settle in, to learn the routine themselves, and be ready to start without distractions the minute the second bell rings. This usually helps but does not solve the problem.

My next course of action is to make posters and signs outlining the morning routine for the students. We discuss these again in class. Such posters usually start with, "After saying goodbye to your parent at the door, . . ." Even this touches off negative feelings. One year a little boy asked his mother to come into the classroom before school to help him and to socialize with him. Mother was hanging at the door watching her son's every move. She replied in a loud voice so I would be sure to hear, "I'm not *allowed* to come in!"

By the end of the first quarter, if I see that a student needs more responsibility for himself and his own learning, I bring it up at the parent-teacher conference. I talk about how proud they will feel when Susie can do more things by herself, how they won't have to phone me or a classmate to find out the homework, how a behavior that is cute now won't be cute when the child is twelve. Most parents acknowledge what they are doing. We discuss techniques such as using timers and letting the child experience consequences. For example, if Susie forgets her lunch, she may go to the office to borrow money to buy school lunch. If she forgets her homework, she stays in a recess to do it, and so on.

The really overinvolved parents will still excuse what they are doing: "But she never eats anything from the school lunch" or "She doesn't eat much breakfast, so she needs to eat her snack at recess!" I explain gently that most first graders eat very little, period. I see how much of their home lunches they throw away or trade, and no one in my class is in danger of being malnourished because of not eating a bit of lunch for a day, although the expensive processed snacks they eat at recess may take the edge off their appetite for lunch.

I must zero in on the parents who want a report on their child almost daily quite quickly, or they think their child is becoming labeled by peers and the school as "bad," that I need to run my classroom differently, or that I am the wrong teacher for their child. First of all, I ask if their student has reported any of the good things that happened in school, and I usually list a few. Surprise! They frequently don't know anything about them. So I direct the parent to ask their child to tell them about the *good* things that happened that day. Very often just doing that changes everything.

If little Johnny still complains of negative things such as the teacher picking on him, work is too hard, teacher doesn't tell me how to spell words, and so on, I instruct the parent to say, "I hear what you are saying. We have talked about that many times and discussed solutions. Unless you do something to solve this problem, I don't want to hear about it anymore." After about two weeks, one boy had become a different and happier child when his mother refused to wallow with him every afternoon after school.

When asked for a daily report, I will be honest. I won't say a child has been an angel if she hasn't been. However, much of what happens is normal behavior for a six-year-old. I certainly wouldn't write or call home about it. I just take care of it at school. In this way, a daily report tends to bring out the negative. So I tell the parents that they will be contacted if something happens that they should know about, but for the child's sake, I will not give a daily report on her behavior. The child needs to make her own decisions, and some of them will be wrong. That's okay! The pressure of a daily report in some instances causes the child to make wrong decisions on purpose just because the decisions are then hers, not her parents or the teachers. When I explain this to parents and they back off, again, I have seen children start to make good decisions on their own.

Many people think that teaching in a school with an upper-middle-class population is a dream. In so many ways, it is. As teachers, though, we also have to keep in mind our school vision and our state General Learner Outcomes: We teach the whole child. The student should be able to work independently, to recognize good work, to work collaboratively with others, and to solve problems. For this to happen, our students need to be able to appreciate what they have, manage their belongings, and be willing to face a challenge and solve simple problems. Overinvolved parents often deprive their children of these experiences in their daily lives. Teachers can sometimes be a catalyst in these situations, and I can see no better place to start than in first grade where the academics kick in over and beyond their daily and family activities.

CHAPTER 23

Grantwriting Tips to Accommodate Learners' Needs

Teresa Morton Owens

Blountsville, Alabama

A s a fifth-grade teacher in a rural school system in Alabama, I don't have to explain much to inform you of the educational funding in my state. As a math teacher, I've often wondered how a close-to-zero amount can be prorated. My educational guess is that when you have *nothing* this year, they'll extend that *nothing* to next year, too. We can laugh all day long, but it still will not help your situation.

You want and need great things for your classroom. You're tired of using your own money to pay for it, and you don't want to ask your students' parents, because they don't have it to spare. Sure, you may get classroom instructional money to the tune of a paltry $400 for the year, but how far will that go toward the purchase of technology items? How many businesses can start up with $400 for the year? I don't know of any, other than the local lemonade stand. So you have a dilemma: You do without, pay for it yourself, or write a grant. It's your decision.

The plausible solution is to write a grant. In the next few paragraphs, I share some of my grantwriting tips with you.

Where is this money going to come from? Shop online for available grants. Be sure to check for deadline dates. Usually, it is a good idea to set up a calendar to remind you when a specific grant is due. I try to use a year time frame. I shop at the beginning of the school year for grants that I would like to apply to by the following spring. Then I can be aware of specific classroom needs during the school year. There are many grants available out there from charitable foundations. Do not get hooked into the scam of sending money to a phony foundation to get a list of grants. There are plenty of scams out there as well. Be cautious and use your brain. Always check out suspicious companies and foundations. Do your research.

After you have shopped for grants, the first step is to find out what it is that you need. Think big. Assess your classroom. Ask yourself, "What do I need to help specific populations of my students?" Do you have ELL (English language learners) or first-year English learners, students with attention deficit/hyperactivity disorder (ADD/ADHD), students who are shy, or students who are bullies? How much time does it take to interact with students to help them understand? What could you use to make it easier? Assessing your classroom population should be the initial focus, before research. Without knowing exactly what you are trying to accomplish and with whom, spending your precious and nonexistent time would be in vain. I usually target my research to a group that has a specific need. This allows me to plan a prescription. If my proposal is selected, I can also see and measure results more readily, thus making evaluation of my project easier to assess.

I have written grants to assist my ELL and ADD/ADHD kids by purchasing books on tape. A grant that enabled me to buy *Math Sharks* helped my students who had poor basic math skills. I even wrote a proposal to assist in purchasing paper for the copier machine to assist the math class, which used the Accelerated Math program. If you have a great enough need and can word the need well enough, your proposal will eventually be selected. It may take a few attempts. You can even write to the grant foundation and ask how you scored. They will be able to give you pointers on problems with your manuscript.

Yes, you have to jump through hoops. If the directions state that all margins should be two inches, make sure you use that measurement. Pay attention to detail and first impressions. If they fax the form to your school, don't just write the information they asked for in pen! Take it from the fax, scan it, and start rejuvenating the form. Then type your information into the form using Microsoft Word. Save it. Proofread. Print it on quality paper. Be ready to do a fantastic job. Remember, someone on the other end has to pick up that paper and read it. Will they feel better about your paper if it looks nice? It shouldn't matter, but it does. Are you impressed when one of your students turns in an immaculate, well-written paper?

Once you've decided on your target area, do your research. How many boys? How many girls? Do they come from single-parent families? Do plotted scores from standardized testing show a decrease in ability level? Is your school a Chapter I school, where more than 50 percent of the students receive the federal free and reduced lunches program? All of these mark a specific need. Even if you have more girls than boys, creative proposals can get money to your classroom so you can teach this group better. Is there a need in the community that your school can adopt as a special project? Collaboration between community and schools is a great selling point for grant proposals. Plus, it benefits your students immensely to share with others from the community. Are there other teachers in your school who share the same needs? Research must prove your need. For instance, you can't say that you need a computer to help the kids in your room on writing if their scores last year were the highest in the district. But chances are, if you have an intense need for your students to be able to write compositions more adeptly, there is another teacher in your school who shares the same need. Collaboration between teachers also demonstrates to the foundation a willingness to complete a project.

After you've decided what you need and you have the data to back it up, start writing. It would be wise to set up a folder, titled "Grants," on your computer desktop. Then set up a file within the folder for each grant. It's also a good idea to scan all application forms and save them to the file. When filling out the necessary forms, never handwrite them (unless specifically requested). After they are scanned, type the information directly onto them through the scanner and save it to MS Word. This way, if your grant is funded, you have access to exactly how you proposed you would carry out the grant endeavor. Many grant applications ask you to chart how you will assess success of the proposed activity.

Naming your grant proposal should never be done without thinking. Aside from the look of your proposal, this is key to making a great impression. A catchy title is often the best. One of my more creative titles came from my bizarre habit of inverting phrases. Taken from the phrase and popular film *Sum of All Fears,* I came up with "Combating the Fear of All Sums." This title helped to establish my purpose of seeking money to purchase math manipulatives for my class. Further, each time I typed the title, I used this font: `Combating the Fear of All Sums`. Be cautious, read all of the directions and requirements. If the grant proposal is to be printed in size 12, using Times New Roman font, make certain that you follow the directions to the "nth" degree. If it allows for creativity, using a font that further illustrates your point can be beneficial.

Jot down brainstorming ideas regarding the activities, procedures, and requirements of your proposal. You will revise this list by excluding any idea that doesn't fit into your topic or cannot be backed up with your rationale and data. Next, place the items in order. Usually this order is dictated by the granting foundation.

After you have checked the order to present your information, start writing. I always type the title or question that I am addressing in bold at the beginning of the paragraph or section. I then emphasize any direct answers to the topic by placing them in bold as well. Usually some demographic data illustrating your school setting are required as an introduction. This is pertinent to formulating a need. Your plea for assistance must be evident in all of your writing, even if your school is in a high-socioeconomic area. You must write to the topic. Perhaps male students outperform their female counterparts in geometry? Even in upper-income areas, a grant is feasible as long as it demonstrates a need.

Following the opening section, most granting institutions require that you state your proposal. Be specific. Make sure that your answer precisely addresses the question. Usually rationale for your request will come in a later section. When you are providing your rationale for your proposal, use research to back up your request.

After you have accomplished the task of providing your evidence, you will be asked to provide a budget for your acquisitions. Check current catalogs for the most recent prices. If the price tends to fluctuate, check with the vendor about possible price increases. You may even be able to get a discounted purchase price, buying in classroom quantities. Most grants require an itemized budget. Be sure to include shipping and handling costs in the total amount.

Usually the final chore in writing a grant proposal will be for you to provide an effective form of evaluation for the activities you have selected. This does not always require some type of test data. Often it can be a survey or an informal assessment of the degree to which you've experienced success with your planned activities.

Finally, keep your responses to the directed items within the limited number of words or pages as stipulated by the proposal instructions. If your response does not adhere to the specs, it will be eliminated. Proofread your proposal carefully, leaving no misaligned columns or misspelled words. Make sure you include the correct number of copies. Most institutions require signatures of your principal and superintendent. To acquire these can take a few days, so plan ahead and make sure you are within your time line, as laid out by the requirements of the grant. Foundation or granting institutions often require you to send a specified number of copies of the complete proposal. Do not fold your document into a legal-size envelope. Place your paper flat inside a large manila envelope.

Print out your addresses on self-adhesive computer labels with your printer. To ensure that the address label doesn't get wet and become illegible, cover them with wide transparent tape. Most institutions will send a notification that they have received your proposal. This will ease your worry about whether it met the required date of receipt. Beware: Some grants set the deadline date according to when it is received at the office, whereas others place the postmarked date as the cutoff. Some grants are submitted via e-mail and file sharing. Make sure you meet the exact time. Does it have to be in to the office at 9:00 A.M. Eastern Time? Check out whether a certain time zone is specified.

After you have completed your task, don't spend all of your time worrying about whether you will receive the grant monies. Put it on the back burner and concentrate on your kids. Be aware of specific needs to which you can tailor another grant opportunity. Always plan for the next grant proposal. Keep a pad handy where you can jot down catchy phrases, special problems, or special equipment needs. On the pad, note all grant opportunities and deadlines. Most education periodicals have a section dedicated to grants. Begin to collect data required for grants from various schoolwide committees. Having these data at hand will keep you ever prepared for the next all-night grantwriting session and will ensure that it's in the mail on time.

CHAPTER 24

A Shared Responsibility

Eric Stemle
Evanston, Wyoming

E ach spring as my students are preparing for their final exams, I give them an additional but important assignment. I ask them to write a letter of self-evaluation addressed to me in which they describe their learning throughout the course. Their evaluations often focus on curricular lessons but just as much on life lessons they have acquired from their experience. A consistent thread runs throughout these letters from year to year, a feeling that together we have created a unique environment. Although I am ultimately responsible for the direction of my classroom, my students report that it is a collaborative effort that creates a strong sense of class. Our success together depends on the commitment made by each and every student, and it is that support for the mission of the class that makes our brief time with one another extraordinary.

Students tell me that when they enter Room 218 at Evanston High School for the first time, they notice that it's different from other rooms in the building. For one thing, the desks are arranged in a circle instead of rows. For another, their teacher stands not at the front of the room but rather in the entrance to greet them with a handshake. It is from that moment of introduction that I seek to build our sense of class. For the remainder of the term, ours is a class like no other, and our approach to classroom management revolves around the idea that we share responsibility in the room. From that first day, I remind my students that "we are all teachers in this room, and that includes all of you. We are all learners in this room, and that includes me." That premise underlies all decisions that we make in the classroom.

The first few days of the course we spend getting to know one another and setting expectations for ourselves as a class. Along with class building and team building, we talk about the dreams we have for our learning and our personal growth. We then discuss ways to create an environment that will help reach our goals. We brainstorm possibilities and decide what's possible given the established procedures of the school. We seek to achieve a balance between individual comfort and a challenging learning structure, and although the kids enjoy throwing out some outlandish ideas in their brainstorming, they eventually arrive at a consensus that sets the stage for exploration the rest of the year.

As the semester proceeds, we develop a shared management scheme, and that includes participation. Because we're all teachers, there is no focal point in the room for student attention. True, I am the lead teacher, but when we are discussing matters in the circle, I sit among peers. The focus is on whoever is addressing the group, and that person is identified as the one in possession of the koosh ball. There are just a few basic rules regarding the koosh. For one, we only give it to someone who requests it—no surprises to the side of the head! For another, we toss it gently. The idea is to facilitate discussion, not to practice our fastballs, so we make every effort to throw the ball so that it can be caught. The koosh ball plays an integral part in our classroom management. Because we're all teachers, there is not a single person in charge of who speaks and who doesn't. Classmates call on one another, and my only interference may be to remind folks to look for those who have their hands up and haven't held the koosh during the period. Occasionally a class will fall into a pattern with a handful of kids participating, and at that point I suggest that they find ways to involve more people in the proceedings. When discussions bog down, I may also pose questions and ask students to discuss their thoughts with a partner for a short time. This gives the kids a chance to explore the question in a more intimate fashion, to try an answer before presenting it to the circle.

As teachers, we realize that we have a responsibility to be ready for each class, to share what we know, and to encourage our classmates to share. This commitment helps us manage the classroom when it comes time to discuss a reading selection. In their evaluation letters, students say that they feel a strong sense of obligation to their colleagues to be prepared to discuss because they appreciate the opportunity to share their views, to teach. Early on, I tell my classes that I will not threaten them to be ready for discussion. Kids say that when they first hear this, they expect an easy time, free from homework or preparation. This notion changes as the semester evolves, as we grow closer together by sharing ideas and stories about ourselves. In time, the kids say that they feel a duty not just to me but to everyone else in the class. Of course, we're talking about teenagers, and there are times when some kids aren't prepared for a circle discussion. At this point, we have a brief class meeting to review our commitment to the class. This works only if we have taken the time to build the sense of class from day one, if everyone accepts the idea that this is a special class that provides great opportunities for self-expression.

The concept of a class full of teachers extends to cooperative teams as well. One of our uses for teams is to critique writing, and as teachers, students realize that they do more than just edit partners' papers. By sharing their drafts, students can also teach writing to their peers. In a team of four, each writer has the chance to read three introductions, three conclusions, and three arguments. While I provide students with guidelines and exemplars on each assignment, in teams they view models created by writers who are engaged in the same stage of the process that they are. This once again reminds students that they have much more to do in the classroom than absorb information—they are active participants.

The management of our classroom goes far beyond my control. Because I share teaching duties with all of my students, we build the environment together. As the kids say in their final letters, our class challenges them because they sense a commitment to one another: to prepare, to share, to encourage one another. By giving up authoritarian control of the classroom, I make way for my students to become more responsible to their classmates and, more important, to themselves. Kids say that because they have frequent and varied opportunities for expression, they develop a more open approach to the ideas and opinions of others. What better environment for learning could we ever create?

Helpful Tips

Managing a classroom without coercion requires patience and faith. Not only must I have faith in my students and be patient with them, but I must also be patient with myself and believe that I can accomplish my goals.

This means waiting for our class to evolve as an organism, to become a dynamic force that lives together as it learns. This is difficult because while some students are quick to trust their classmates, others take longer, and some may never develop that security required to share. As a class, we discuss the benefits of hearing all voices, and although that can be a challenge in a room of twenty-five to thirty people, we seem to get it done. With reticent students, it may involve private conversations or messages in journals in which I encourage participation or seek information so that I may better help the child. As always, we seek a balance between helping kids feel relaxed and challenging them to take risks.

Of course, even with patience and faith and preparation, there are times when our classroom of teachers does not function smoothly. Kids may seem bored, or they may not come ready to participate fully in the class activities. This can lead to frustration on all of our parts, and here is where I take the lead. It's usually a matter of reminding them of what we agreed to do at the beginning of the term. On my "off" days, I do this with a definite edge to my voice; on my "on" days, I do it with a sense of humor. It's fortunate for me as well as my students that I have far more good days than bad!

CHAPTER 25

My Weekly Newsletter

Veronique Paquette

East Wenatchee, Washington

My first year of teaching was an incredible year of learning. I had just completed my student teaching and had been offered a position as a kindergarten teacher. In no way was I prepared for this grade level. My teacher training had focused on elementary education. The elementary education degree began at first grade; we never discussed kindergarten, which was the territory of the early childhood folks. I quickly overcame my fears and jumped headlong into my new position. I was excited and thrilled to be working in the school district where I had been a student.

Fortunately, my master teacher was an incredible woman who guided me through many of the discoveries of a new teacher. The best part was that she herself had taught kindergarten for many years and eased me through many days of happiness and frustration as a beginning teacher. The commencement of the school year went off without much struggle; the children were excited, I was excited, and the greatest secret was that they had no idea how absolutely terrified I really was. Children are so forgiving. I did everything I was supposed to do. The children and

I were having the best time ever. We were all learning, and life seemed good. Until I had to write my first note home to parents. The task at hand was to notify parents about the upcoming Parent Night. All my confidence and self-assurance went right out the window. I had no idea where to begin. I was at a loss. I understood the conventions of grammar and could apply them well. Yet putting together a note to explain important information for parents exceeded my comfort level. I panicked! I procrastinated! As the time drew closer, I bit the bullet and tried to write a letter. As an overachieving perfectionist, this was not a happy experience for me. Finally, I went to my master teacher and begged for help. She gave me some good advice: "Give them the facts and write from your heart." This seemed to make a lot of sense. So off I went. It took me many attempts to have the wording sound just the way I wanted. Eventually, I was able to put together my letter. It was a half-page note with just the bare-bones information. It was not anywhere near what I wanted, but it accomplished the task.

Each time I was in the position to write another letter that year, I toiled through the same process. It was an agonizing experience. In September of my second year of teaching, it became my personal challenge to myself to overcome this fear of writing. I set about finding a way I could consistently let my students' parents know all the crucial information. I attended trainings put on by other kindergarten teachers. An idea was posed that caught my attention and seemed to be the perfect answer to my dilemma. A newsletter! The teachers I listened to suggested various methods. I decided to create a weekly letter.

At first, I wrote the letter by hand. I would begin writing early in the week and include all the items I believed the parents would want to know: concepts learned, upcoming events, birthdays, and holidays. I would write my letter several times before I finally had a finished copy. I decorated the page with rubber stamps, graduating to clip art as I improved. My master teacher was still there, and she proofread every letter. What a gift it was to have her do this! She found things I missed, sentences that didn't make sense, and generally assisted me by editing.

Now, seventeen years later, I am still writing my weekly newsletter and am not afraid of the writing at all. I have a standard format that I follow when I write my letter. I always begin with the thematic unit

I am teaching and include fun facts the children have learned. The next few paragraphs always pertain to the skills and concepts we are collectively working on in the classroom. The last part of the letter includes any information that parents need to know about field trips, class gatherings, upcoming units, or projects with which we need assistance. The format is always the same, and I follow it religiously, hoping it will elicit good conversation with the families at home. I even try to slip little questions in for the parents to ask their children. Although my master teacher is no longer teaching and is unable to proofread my letters, a dear friend and teaching partner now reads for me.

My ability to put these letters together has grown from handwritten and rubber-stamped letters to computerized letters that go home over the Internet. I send the letter home every Friday in the form of a hard copy and also as an e-mail.

I have discovered that the parents appreciate letting them know what we are doing in the classroom. When I became a parent, my own child's teacher would send periodic newsletters home. I discovered how invaluable these words were. I always knew what was happening in the class without really being there. As a working parent who cannot participate in the classroom with my daughter, those words became my lifeline to her days as a student.

Parents ask all the right questions of their children when the school day is done, and children answer as honestly as they can—most often with the same response, "Nothing" or "I don't remember." Newsletters let parents know about their child's learning in a broad and general way. They allow the students the freedom to have ownership of their learning while allowing parents the knowledge that they are in a classroom where great things are happening in their child's life.

CHAPTER 26

Success Is Just a Click Away!

Beverly R. Plein

Cresskill, New Jersey

C hris moved around the classroom in a carefree manner while the other students worked quietly and diligently on their tasks. In other classes, Chris would often get in trouble because he could not sit still, did not know how or when to take notes, and could not complete assignments according to the directions written on the board. Group work was a nightmare. Chris's classmates hardly ever picked him to be in their group; he was not perceived as being bright because he could not focus and was not reliable when it came to completing assignments. Chris appeared incapable and uninterested in learning, and consequently most teachers had low expectations for him.

Striving for excellence is a goal that every student should be encouraged to work toward in all aspects of their lives. Learning new ideas to the best of one's abilities, becoming a better person, and making a contribution to one's community can mean improved outcomes for every student. Teachers should promote excellence. In theory, the individual education plan (IEP) is designed for that very purpose. Created by a team of learning experts, the IEP should help the teacher become aware of the student's weaknesses while identifying the tools and methods of assistance that will serve to strengthen that child's role in the learning process. Core curriculum standards and standardized testing often determine the amount and type of knowledge that each student should possess about a specific topic.

The classroom teacher should determine the appropriate learning activities and assessments based on the individual abilities and experiences of the students in the classroom. Learning to ask questions such as What does the student need to know?, Why does he or she need to know this information?, and How will this information be relevant to that student in the future? may be one of the most important facets to planning successful learning experiences for the student with learning disabilities, as well as the other students in the class. For the mainstreamed teacher, the IEP can serve as a map with clearly marked roadways as well as obstacles to avoid in the learning process.

Chris had difficulty with written tests, but he loved using computers. He knew things about computers that other students did not and enjoyed playing on the computer for hours. While other students were given topics to write about, Chris was given the digital camera and told to take a picture that illustrated a specific example of something that was learned in class. After he found the image he was looking for, he felt successful and was excited to hear the next assignment. By dividing the assignment into small tasks, Chris was able to have many successful experiences within one class period and remained focused and productive. During the next class, Chris was given a list of questions that needed to be answered in his project but was not given specific instructions as to how it should be done. Discussion of possibilities sparked his interest.

Engaging Chris in the learning experience enabled him to take ownership of his learning. Because he was in control of the outcome, he was able to create something meaningful with the knowledge that he had obtained in class. Once provided with the tools he needed, Chris was developing strategies to become an independent thinker. Infusing technology in the classroom allows a teacher to meet the needs of all students because learning can become individualized. Students do not need to hear lectures about the vastness of the universe, but rather can see this vastness for themselves by looking at images directly from satellites orbiting the earth. Instead of reading about important events in a history book, students can read primary-source documents and come to their own conclusions. Students can discover the world around them by accompanying scientists on their explorations, viewing real-time data and imagery.

Viewing photos of World War II soldiers while listening to music from the era helps to bring the period alive. All students do not need to take the same path to gain knowledge. The Internet allows students to travel the information highway at their own speed.

Some students will travel quickly, simply completing assignments; others will take their time and explore those things about which they are passionate. Teachers need to take an active role in the process by completing a "pretrip" to make sure the destinations will be educational and appropriate.

Teachers have an obligation to make learning meaningful and to prepare students of all abilities for the world that lies ahead. One lesson that should be the central force of all learning is a can-do attitude. Students need to believe in themselves and their abilities to be successful members of society. In September when a teacher looks at the roster, he or she does not know what special talents and interests the students listed there may possess. Perhaps more important than creating beautiful bulletin boards or classroom newsletters is to take the time to get to know one's students and their interests. Design lesson plans that relate directly to their passions, encourage them to develop dreams, and help them find the path to fulfill them.

A well-managed classroom is about providing opportunities for laughter and for success. It is about encouraging students to support one another as they work in teams on assignments and share their knowledge. It is about allowing the sounds of chaos and ignoring rumbles of enthusiasm as students discover new ideas. It is about taking time to recognize the brightness of a smile that comes when a student has met his goal or giving a student a nod of approval when she sighs with pleasure from an accomplishment. It is about realizing when a student needs a boost of encouragement and when a student needs to complete a task on his or her own. It is about determining the best way for each student to learn and then to provide that opportunity whenever possible. Creating a classroom environment that inspires excellence and provides appropriate learning experiences for students of all abilities is perhaps the quintessential classroom management tool.

Helpful Tips

Directly inside the classroom door I have posted an assignment chart for the students to keep track of which homework assignments they have turned in and received credit for. Before passing back the assignments, the student who finishes an assignment early or needs something to do places a sticker by each person's name that has a graded paper. Students can check the chart at their convenience, be that before and after school or during lunchtime. Guidance counselors, special education teachers, and teacher aides can also see the chart if they want to keep making sure a student has completed all the assignments.

In addition, one of the students files all the extra copies of worksheets in file folders (labeled appropriately) and stores them in a file holder next to the assignment chart. A student is able to determine the assignment he or she is missing and can get a worksheet without even stepping into the classroom. Students are anxious to see stickers by their name and eagerly take the responsibility to complete their assignments. I also keep track of extra credit on the same chart. With this method, students assume responsibility for their work without additional effort on my part.

CHAPTER 27

Ideas to Help Students Thrive in a Stimulating and Successful Learning Environment

Pam Roller

Galveston, Indiana

I t is my firm belief that teachers make a difference by being role models, setting good examples, and instilling a desire for students to learn each day in the classroom. Creating a stimulating and successful classroom learning environment enhances lives! Within the classroom setting, teachers have a choice and an opportunity to make today better than yesterday, and tomorrow better than today. I have a passion for creating a learning environment that allows each child to experience a great deal of success because success breeds success. Students learn best and discover new things when they are allowed to be curious, think, explore, experiment, ask questions, imagine, and dream.

Since 1988, my classroom has had the acronym SMILES, INC. It stands for Success, Motivation, Incredible experiences, Love, Encouragement, and Support, which produces Incredibly Neat Children! Each day in SMILES, INC., the students recite a daily oath that holds them accountable for doing their personal best, following the rules, and choosing to make the day a good day. This procedure works because the students make choices to make our classroom environment a safe, secure, positive place. SMILES, INC. is a success. I have had parents tell me that their children do not want to stay home, even when they are ill. I have had them say that their children would go to school on Saturday and Sunday if I offered it. One parent told me that they were going to Walt Disney World for a vacation, and it would involve an extension of the school's spring vacation by a few days. Her daughter was not happy about missing school. The little girl asked her mother whether they could take Miss Roller with them. I did not go on the trip, but the little girl called me from Florida to tell me she missed me and that she loved me.

We have a funeral to bury "I can't" in the school courtyard. This is done the first week of school because these two words keep us from accomplishing all we can. This experience helps the students get rid of the negative, and it helps them focus on the positive. The students and the teacher write down several "I can'ts." A funeral is planned, sometimes with or without a minister, and the "I can'ts" are buried in the school courtyard. A big rock with "I can't" written on it reminds everyone not to use "I can't" again. Those words are replaced with "I can," "I will," and "I want to."

After leaving the courtyard, the students and the teacher return to the classroom to write down goals for the first semester, the school year, and for life, using the positive words "I can," "I will," and "I want to." Then we take action to try to achieve our goals. These goals are kept in a special file folder and given back to the students on the last day of the school year. The students are amazed at how many goals they have achieved. A parent commented one day while she was volunteering in my classroom, "'I can't' is working! My daughter won't let us use 'I can't' at home either." My students are expected to write at least one or two things in their journals daily for which they are grateful. No matter what happened at home the night before, in the morning before school starts, or on the way to school, my students have it instilled in them that they always have something to be grateful for.

If they write down what they are grateful for, their attitudes change from negative to positive. School is often a safe haven for children. I cannot control what happens to my students beyond my classroom, but while they are in my care, I choose to create a happy classroom climate that enables students to love learning and to feel loved, accepted, and included.

Creating an extraordinary environment excites and stimulates learning. Part of my classroom looks like a jungle and includes a life-size tree house with a hammock, several seven-foot trees, lots of realistic-looking stuffed animals from the rain forest, a lagoon, and classroom pets, including a tortoise from South America, a talking parrot, a tarantula, a hedgehog, fish, and frogs. The other part of my classroom has a room-size space shuttle simulator with a mission control center. In addition to focusing on the basic skills and state standards, my students are stimulated by growing lots of plants, watching chicks hatch, and growing their own butterflies; they learn valuable lessons by watching our ant farm, and taking care of pets teaches them responsibility. I truly believe that students understand more when they are actively involved in the learning process.

My classroom is child-centered, and each child is showcased for a week with a bulletin board called "Under the Kapok Tree." Just as the great kapok tree is important to many plants, insects, and animals in the rain forest, my students are important to me and in their world. They bring in photos of themselves and their family, as well as personal treasures and other items that are valuable to them. Attached to the bulletin board is a special paper with a list of nice things each of the classmates said about them. They can keep it forever and remember, on a day when they are feeling lonely or sad, that they are loved.

Parental involvement is a key factor in the success of my students. I teach many of our "at-risk" and academically and behaviorally challenged students. Several of their parents have had bad school experiences or feel intimidated by educators, and they choose to stay away from school, even when it comes to their own children's education.

Through God's grace I have reached all the parents of my students over the years—not just at parent-teacher conferences but by including and involving the parents in my own School On Saturday Program. School On Saturday offers my students and their parents an opportunity to engage together in meaningful and fun learning activities. I integrate the curriculum using a hands-on approach and apply what the students are learning to real-life situations.

By using their imagination, they have simulated Space Shuttle missions, designed landings for a Mars egg drop, flown to the rain forest, went snorkeling in the high school swimming pool to learn about the ocean, gone horseback riding, canoeing, and so on. I am a world traveler and a lifelong learner who loves to share with my students, colleagues, and community. For twenty-eight years, I have planned an imaginary trip around the world. My students learn words from five languages, wear costumes, sing, and dance. Students write their parents to invite them to travel around the world with us. The room is filled with displays and mementos from around the world. The parents and their children board an imaginary jet, and they learn together as they travel the world. Food is served representing different countries. This is the finale of the school year. By this time, not only are the students and their parents hooked, but I have grandparents attending as well. One year, a little special education student could never get her mother to come to school for anything. Before the year was over, her mother chaperoned a field trip and brought Grandma to our trip around the world. Once inside my classroom, the mother and grandmother didn't want to leave and expressed why it was difficult for them to come to school. They felt illiterate, and it was easier for them to stay home than to face teachers who did not understand them. If you can understand children, you can reach their parents, and that enables success.

Even though many of my students are "at risk," they are challenged to learn the basic skills and meet the state standards. I have great expectations for them with a vision of each of my students reaching his or her fullest potential. I will go the distance for each child. A fascinating learning environment is created for my students. Each year, I challenge myself to come up with some outrageous project to help my students learn and remember forever. I try to find out my students' interests and incorporate what they like into our reading and writing curriculum whenever possible. When the students realize you care enough about them to show an interest in the things they like, teaching is easy and learning is fun.

My students learn the importance of encouragement. I tell them the greatest thing they can do in this life is to encourage someone and that this will make the world a better place. My students not only encourage one another, they cheer one another on throughout the day, on a daily basis, all year long. It may sound silly, but it really creates an atmosphere of positive feelings and gives hope to those little guys who would rather give up.

It does not matter which area of the curriculum I am teaching; integrating is what I do, and I use all five senses if possible. My students learn by doing. They are constantly engaged in the learning process, and I instill in them that when they participate in the learning process, they understand information better and remember it longer. Here is an example. I spend a great deal of time teaching phonics. It is the foundation of learning to read. I want my students to know that reading is not just in books and on worksheets, so after learning all of the vowel sounds and vowel combinations, I have taken my students on a shopping trip to a local supermarket. To have money to shop with, we made our own lip balm and sold it. We went to the supermarket, and the students shopped for items using their decoding skills to purchase groceries needed for the Ronald McDonald House in Indianapolis. We also bought sheets and towels at Wal-Mart. Before this experience, my students did not get the connection that to buy things from the store, they had to be able to read the packages and labels. We were allowed to take a field trip to the Ronald McDonald House to deliver our items and see the house that love built. It had an impact on my kids.

If students can read and write, they can succeed. When we are growing plants, hatching chicks, learning metamorphosis by growing butterflies, watching ants work together to build colonies, simulating missions in space, recycling, traveling around the world, building kites, or designing bottle rockets, I provide hundreds of books for my students to read. They in turn go to the library to check out books on whatever topic we are learning. I require my students to write about the interesting things we do in class, but they do not mind because the experiences they have had are fascinating to them. Since 1995, my students have participated in the Trucker Buddy International Program. They got to be writing pals while improving in grammar and learning geography through the eyes of a trucker. We mapped and graphed all the states he traveled and displayed the letters, postcards, and mementos from around the United States on a huge bulletin board. It was better than filling in blanks in a workbook. It gave us a purpose for writing, and it was neat to get responses each month. We were fortunate to have our trucker buddies visit our school.

During the past three years, my students have published four class books through Nationwide Learning in Topeka, Kansas. Each student authored and illustrated pages in the books. This experience gave them a great sense of accomplishment and culminated a year's work of applying reading and writing skills. It motivated them to learn and gave them a sense of ownership. Our books are available for checkout at our school library and at the county library. The school librarian said our books are always checked out, and the director of the county library showed great admiration for my students' contributions to the library. After the attack on the United States in September 2001, we honored our country with a book titled *Proud to Be Americans* and published a book called *We Can Save the Earth!* These two books were sent to the White House library. My students will always remember the hard work it took to publish the books, and they will be able to share them with their children and grandchildren someday. My students have also been selected to have their poems published in the Anthology of Poetry by Young Americans for 2002 and 2003.

Every year since 1991, I have collaborated with the sixth graders in our school. They have been paired up individually to work with my second graders as sixth-grade buddies. The sixth graders come every Monday and Wednesday morning for fifteen minutes. Together they practice reading the story we have in reading class for the week, practice vocabulary words, read library books, and practice the spelling words for the week. Because about 35 percent of my students are "at risk," I have to find different ways to help each child reach his or her fullest potential. This experience has provided each student with a positive person two days a week on whom they can depend to help them academically. When the sixth graders take turns reading stories with my students, it provides my students with someone else in their lives, other than their teacher or parents, who can read with good expression. I train the sixth graders to encourage my second graders.

The sixth graders have to fill out a buddy form before they leave my classroom, which holds them accountable for working with my students, and it makes them more responsible. Many of them write very encouraging remarks on the forms. The encouragement given makes each one of my students want to try harder, and they look forward to their sixth-grade buddy coming again. My students are held accountable for their behavior as far as listening and cooperating with the sixth-grade buddies. The forms are sent home each Monday and Wednesday so the parents can see that an extra effort was made helping their child with reading and spelling skills. For thirteen years, my students have been the winners in this learning experience. Their reading and spelling skills always improve tremendously. These are the students who would normally fall through the cracks if they did not have the consistent help from our sixth-grade buddies. My students score higher on state standardized tests with the regular help of a sixth-grade buddy than if they did not receive the extra help at all. It was hard for my students to read books for fun when they could not read well. Because of the extra time spent with the sixth graders, reading library books or books for the Scholastic Reading Counts Program, my second graders learn to enjoy reading for pleasure. The neatest thing to see is how excited the second graders get when they are able to read chapter books. The sixth graders are trained to ask the second graders questions throughout the books being read. This helps my students greatly with reading comprehension. In the Scholastic Reading Counts Program, my students read books, then take quizzes, by themselves, on the computer to check their reading comprehension.

Two-thirds of my students score above and beyond the points expected of them as second graders. My special education students and those with learning disabilities always go beyond what is expected of them as well. This is because I believe in setting high standards, having great expectations for my students, and involving the sixth-grade buddies in my class every year. Over the years, the sixth graders have designed their own games for the second graders to play. This experience gives the sixth graders an opportunity to be creative and is a fun way for the second graders to practice reading and spelling skills. The games have been really interesting and unique and have included game boards and game markers or tokens to play the games.

The sixth graders have benefited as well, because they have had an opportunity to help make a difference in someone else's life. The sixth graders get to witness the progress the second graders made throughout the year. They are positive role models for my students. When we cannot meet for some reason (one class or the other was on a field trip), the students miss each other. The sixth-grade teacher has commented over the years that this experience has been valuable for her students as well as for mine. I am truly grateful for this teacher's willingness to let her students collaborate with mine. Over the years, many of my students have looked forward to becoming sixth-grade buddies. It has been wonderful to have former second graders working in my room as sixth-grade buddies. Having sixth-grade buddies has truly made a difference in the lives of my students.

At the end of the year, when I ask my second graders to write down the things we did during the year that they enjoyed the most, many have mentioned having a sixth-grade buddy; writing to our trucker buddy; authoring, illustrating, and publishing books; publishing poems; and having an opportunity to learn with their parents during School On Saturday. They always indicate how much they loved being in a class called SMILES, INC., where they were constantly engaged in a fascinating learning environment that motivated, excited, and stimulated them to think, question, imagine, dream, explore, and discover new things. Most important, they felt loved, accepted, and they accomplished many things.

CHAPTER 28

Strategies Over the Years

Joyce Dunn

Shanksville, Pennsylvania

I t is eight o'clock. The bell rings, and into my classroom burst the children arriving at school on the first buses. I am instantly swamped with bus notes, cafeteria money, milk money, stories of things that happened on the bus, and accounts of events in the lives of my first graders.

"Mrs. Dunn, I left my lunch bag on the bus, and I don't like the spaghetti the cafeteria is having today."

"Mrs. Dunn, did you know my mom grounded me for eight years?"

From that moment on, the day blends from one activity to another, and it does not end until the last child boards a bus at the end of the day.

There are few, if any, minutes during the day to prepare activities, organize materials, check papers, and so on. Teachers are, perhaps, the busiest people in the world, not only during the workday but also in their daily lives, managing family commitments, continuing education, and community involvement. Time is a precious resource that must be used wisely. The better organized the teacher, the smoother the school day will run. In my opinion, the key to good classroom management begins with preparation and organization.

Preventative strategies will take care of most behavior problems. When a class is highly organized, flowing smoothly from task to task, children are less likely to become bored or have extra time to act out. A few strategies I have found that have helped me over the years are the following.

On top of my desk each morning, I have seat work to pass out as soon as the children arrive. For example, comprehension is a skill that can be continually reinforced. Reading passages with accompanying comprehension questions are waiting for the students when they come in. As they practice the reading and begin easing into the day's activities, I have time to do the never-ending housekeeping chores for the morning. When my tasks are finished, we review the reading together.

To help keep myself and the class orderly when I am absent, on top of my desk I have a plastic crate about six inches high. In this crate, I have a substitute folder that contains things such as

- Class list
- Schedule
- Special classes
- Special teachers who will be coming into the room
- Medical information
- Early/emergency dismissal information
- Attendance forms
- Milk and lunch information
- Where special items are located

This information is not only invaluable to the substitute, but it saves me time and paperwork when I return to class.

Also in the crate I keep five laminated folders, each marked with a day of the week. In the folder, I place the papers that will be used along with other materials for the day. I refill this folder for the next week on Friday.

In the crate, I keep a folder full of story webs, Venn diagrams, basic math facts, story starters, and so on, that can be adapted to any lesson by me or by a substitute. This ensures that even those extra five or ten minutes at the end of class are always filled with productive practices. Students who are on task with meaningful activities are less likely to find someone to wrestle with or make a mess! During a hectic day, it is essential that important information is located quickly. To ensure that valuable time is not lost searching for that information, I keep the following items on top of my desk:

■ Lesson plans
■ Attendance forms
■ Milk money/lunch details
■ Schedule
■ Manuals to be used

To save time in my planning, I make and copy a generic lesson plan that I use weekly. It contains information such as class times, subjects, special classes, and any other procedures that would change weekly. I leave space for objectives, methods of instruction, pages, and daily lessons. At the top of the plans, I put the name of the teacher manuals and student workbooks as well as the location where they can be found.

Of course, teachers are not limited to day-to-day activities. There are always those additional commitments and events that occur weekly, monthly, and yearly. In a filing cabinet, I mark important materials in folders that are used year after year. Having this information easily accessible at any time allows you to be prepared for any additional task, even on the busiest of days.

Some suggestions for these folders include the following:

■ Field trip information (permission slips, directions, previous trips, office forms)
■ Testing information (practice tests, rubrics)
■ Inservice information (handouts, articles)
■ Grade sheets
■ Beginning-of-the-year information (before-school preparations)
■ End-of-the-year information (book inventory, requisition forms)
■ Scheduling information

- Class list
- Parent night information

Even with the best-laid and -executed plans, some students will finish early. In the beginning of the year, I instruct my students on how to write letters to one another and how to work independently at work centers. If a student completes his or her work before others, he or she then knows to continue working on an independent learning experience.

Around the room I have individual mailboxes marked with each child's name. There a student can place letters he or she has written to classmates in his or her free time. The content of the letter is up to the child! This helps to foster a sense of creativity in individual students in addition to creating a sense of community. The boxes can also be used to distribute papers to be taken home to the parents, messages, and letters from the teacher and pen pals.

Possible centers for independent work include the following:

- *Art center.* Art materials such as paints, glue, scissors, construction paper
- *Listening center.* Tape recorders, ear phones, tapes, writing materials
- *Math center.* Math fact cards, math games, counters, number lines, worksheets
- *Computer center.* Computer disks
- *Writing center.* Paper, pencils, markers, materials for making books
- *Reading center.* Comfortable chairs, magazines, class books (use color-coded stickers marking reading levels on books)

Update the centers continually with new materials and activities so students will find the independent lessons interesting and valuable, not just busy work.

My final, but every bit as crucial, bit of organizing advice is to dejunk the room! Throw out or give away anything not used in the past year. Keep only what is needed, and label what is there. This will help not only you but also a substitute or anyone covering your class.

Helpful Tip

Have you ever looked at your room as if you were coming into it as a substitute teacher? Could you find materials? Are plans easy to follow? Is your classroom organized and streamlined? If you take the time to organize, declutter, prioritize, and label, the ease of classroom management will improve one-hundred-fold.

CHAPTER 29

A Community of Learners

Cathy Lutz

Madison, Mississippi

If you were to peek through the window in our classroom door, you would see a very diverse group of first graders. Of the twenty-two students in my self-contained class, eleven are boys, eleven are girls. Several races and ethnicities are represented—African American, Indian, Asian, Middle Eastern, Caucasian, Hispanic. Along with the rich cultural heritages present in the classroom, we also have a wide range of academic abilities. Two students are considerably below and six are significantly above grade level in mathematics and reading.

Even so, they are typical of peers their same age cognitively and socially. They are enthusiastic, enjoy a lot of activities, and are eager to please. This class loves to ask questions, likes to review learning, and needs closure. They have a limited attention span and cannot sit still for much longer than fifteen minutes. I have divided my classroom into sections, including areas for reading, mathematics, and science and a large area for group meetings. I usually plan our group meetings extensively; however, being self-contained, we can spontaneously conduct them as needs arise. It is through our group meetings that we build a community of learners. It is imperative to begin the school year with a plan to develop a sense of community through group meetings. This plan should be implemented on the first day of school and is to be developed throughout the entire school year.

We begin each day with our Morning Meeting. During this time, I use teacher-planned and children-directed activities to develop a sense of community among our class of learners. We begin our Morning Meeting with music and movement activities. We sing three songs, such as "This Land Is Your Land, This Land Is My Land," "What Is the Weather Today?" and "Tell Me in the Morning," recorded by Hap Palmer. Next, we select a partner and perform a dance and clap routine to "Zip-pe-de-Do-Dah!" Students rotate daily as student of the day and act as our Morning Meeting leader. The student of the day leads us as we complete myriad calendar and mathematics activities, including a "question of the day." The students use a two-column graph and picture–name cards to answer a yes-or-no question about themselves, and we discuss the data collected. Next, the student of the day moves to the center of our group, and we form a compliment circle around him or her. I begin by giving the student a compliment. For example, I may say, "Shanna, I really liked the way you illustrated the story you wrote in your journal yesterday. You used a lot of details!" Then, beginning on my left and continuing clockwise, each student will give Shanna a compliment.

The purpose is to build a sense of community. We all love to get a compliment. This helps develop students' ability to accept compliments and provides them with practice giving sincere compliments to someone else. During this process of learning how to give and receive, we form deep, emotional bonds with one another. Finally, we share a story and end with our schoolwide pledge, the Madison Station PAWS pledge: "As a Madison Station Jaguar, I am Preparing, Aiming, and Working for Success. Today I will treat others with kindness and respect."

I also plan thematic units designed to promote a community of learners. We begin the year with a unit titled, "We Are All Alike, We Are All Different." This allows us to make connections and develop an appreciation for our differences. These skills must be continually modeled and deliberately taught to children. It is especially important for young children because as they are becoming less self-absorbed, they begin to notice similarities and differences in others. They must be taught that different is just different—not better or worse. This also helps foster a celebration for our own differences and helps promote a society more tolerant and accepting of all others. By modeling respect for diversity and by planning specific learning instances in which these differences are duly noted and clearly respected, a safe and secure environment is established for all students.

To facilitate building classroom community, I pool from a variety of sources. We read aloud, share our art projects, share our journal writings, and have many specific and general classroom discussions. We use the following resources and procedures to facilitate discussions.

There is an abundance of quality literature available, such as Kevin Henkes's *Chrysanthemum* and Shel Silverstein's *The Giving Tree.* These, along with numerous others, lend themselves to open and nonthreatening discussions about character education.

My school, Madison Station Elementary, is part of the Whole Schools Institute, which means we integrate the arts into all subject areas. Our principal, Beverly Johnston, provides professional development training to teachers on how to integrate the arts. A visiting artist, Kay Thomas, wrote "Miss Kay's Rules of Art." These rules focus mainly on art appreciation. Some examples are the following: Every piece of art is about an idea; art means taking a risk; try to think of a new way to do something. Another rule that is quite comforting to young children is that it doesn't have to look real to be art. This allows the most timid student a willingness to try and not to be afraid to create because he or she cannot make it look "just right." The comfort level in my classroom is so great that children feel they can create, talk about, and share anything.

We use Edward de Bono's "Six Thinking Hats for Schools" to facilitate our group discussions. This method is valuable when talking about any subject. In the Six Hats method, thinking is divided into six modes, represented by different-colored hats. The red hat is used for feelings and emotions, the green hat for new ideas and creativity, the yellow hat for thinking about good points, and the black hat is for thinking about bad points. The white hat is used for facts and information, and the blue hat is for thinking about thinking. The purpose is to get children to use all six modes of thinking. The Six Hats method allows children to think more richly and comprehensively. The hats supply cues and allow for open-ended responses.

Children are able to become more self-directed as the hats provide a framework for organized thinking. Thinking then becomes more focused and more constructive. The children become so familiar with using the thinking hats that they can easily interchange them and flow effortlessly from one to the other.

Another equally important procedure used to support student learning and to build classroom community is TAG. When the students are sharing writing pieces or pieces of art, we frequently "play TAG." TAG is a strategy I learned from Dr. Cathy Stewart at a professional development session. It is an acronym for "Tell me what you liked; Ask a question; Give some suggestions." This puts the students in control of the discussion and allows them to work closely with their peers as they compliment and value one another's work. Because this activity is student driven, they are not limited to my questions, but instead ask thought-provoking questions and come up with suggestions that are on their personal levels. Another value of TAG is that the students are really and truly learning to listen to one another and to accept or reject suggestions courteously, all while feeling respected in a safe environment.

For example, a recent journal entry a child shared with the class during TAG began, "My life is hard. I have two houses." When she shared her writing, the class listened intently with compassion. They wanted to learn more about how she handled the situation. This encouraged other students to write about their personal living situations. She openly discussed the confusing and hurtful feelings she had about being a product of a divorced family and about living in two houses. One of the questions asked was, "How do you live in two houses?" She explains her visitation schedule. She also discusses hearing her parents fight. She tells the class it is hard to keep up with where she will be staying. When yet another student asked her which house she likes best, she had a wonderful answer. She said, "Well, I can't really say which one I like the best. My mom's a great mom and my dad's a great dad." That statement could possibly help another student cope who may be going through a similar situation. If not for TAG, we would never have had such a meaningful discussion. Because of the community we had built in our room, she felt comfortable enough and safe enough in this class to share an obviously painful memory. She knew she could trust her peers. All students listened, and all were interested.

In summary, I have discussed several strategies any classroom teacher could use to build classroom community. Having a classroom community of learners eliminates most discipline problems. Students interact with one another in a safe, secure environment. Peer tutoring is automatic. A true sense of "All for One and One for All" is evident! Students take responsibility for their own learning and make sure no friend is left behind.

Helpful Tips

- *Routines.* Establish predictable and reliable classroom routines.
- *Morning Meetings.* Begin each day with a warm and fuzzy "It's great to be here! I can't wait to get started and can't wait to see what the day will bring!" kind of meeting.
- *Compliments.* Give sincere compliments to each student. Never rush through, and never skip this part of your morning routine! Never let a student pass on giving a compliment to the student receiving the compliments. Compliments should never be about physical attributes of the child.
- *Art.* Integrate art into all subject areas. Think of the theory of multiple intelligence research and how you can meet all students' needs. The work of Howard Gardner is a great resource here.
- *Thinking Hats.* After reading de Bono's Six Thinking Hats, create a poster using inexpensive, plastic hats and display them in your meeting area. This will help you to remember to use his highly effective method.
- *TAG.* Make a poster with the acronym "TAG" written vertically (Tell what you liked; Ask a question; Give a suggestion). Then write the explanation beside each letter for a visual reminder to play TAG.

Index

**CORWIN
PRESS**

The Corwin Press logo—a raven striding across an open book—represents the union of courage and learning. Corwin Press is committed to improving education for all learners by publishing books and other professional development resources for those serving the field of K–12 education. By providing practical, hands-on materials, Corwin Press continues to carry out the promise of its motto: **"Helping Educators Do Their Work Better."**